PENDA, Heathen King of Mercia:

His Anglo Saxon world.

By Pete Jennings

1st Edition 2013

2nd Edition 2014

Text & Pictures: Gruff Books © 2013

Dedicated to my old comrade, Gerald 'Aldred' Judge, a true Pecsæton.

Visit Pete Jennings Webpages at
www.gippeswic.demon.co.uk

See Pete Jennings author Page on Amazon
www.amazon.co.uk

Follow Pete Jennings on Facebook

Chapter 1 Why Penda?

Why write a book about a book about a long dead Mercian King? The simple answer is that I was intrigued by odd references to him, and their contradictory nature. Nobody else seems to have brought them together to try and make sense of them, and I enjoy Anglo Saxon history, both in the academic sense and as an historic re-enactor. As a regular performer of living history at Sutton Hoo, Suffolk I have previously been most interested in studying the Wuffing dynasty of East Anglia, but inevitably their relationships with the kingdom of Mercia are an important factor in their story. Under Penda and his sons, Mercia developed into being a major kingdom within Anglo Saxon England, and restricted the domination of others such as Northumbria. That much we can safely deduce, but I will be the first to admit that there are many gaps in the collective knowledge, and consequently I may have ended up asking more questions than I have answered. That is the nature of the beast, but also part of its mysterious appeal. I also wanted to put his life into a wider context of the conditions and customs of his 7th century world.

I am indebted to many people and organisations for both helping me in my research and firing my interest. Dr. Sam Newton, in one of his marvellous Wuffing Education lecture days at Sutton Hoo first commented that nobody seems to have made a focussed literary study on Penda in the same way that he himself had done for King Raedwald of East Anglia.

My fellow members of *Ealdfaeder Anglo Saxons* who re-enact the living history of the times at Sutton Hoo, West Stow (plus the wonderful staff at both sites) and elsewhere inevitably contribute to my thinking around the campfire. *Ða Engliscan Gesiþas* (The English Companions) have whetted my interest with articles in their magazine *Wiþowinde* and website discussions, as have fellow Anglo Saxon enthusiasts at the *Sutton Hoo Society* and individuals Stephen Pollington, Paul Mortimer, Ken Rochester, Linden Currie & Ian Haygreen. Thanks also to Paul and Christine Wilmot and the Heathen Alliance for hospitality and guidance at Hatfield Chase.

Dating

All dating is for the Common Era (CE) but is often contradictory according to the text consulted, or even within the same text. Some scholars believe that Bede's dating is suspect because he started the New Year in September. Some Welsh text dates seem improbable, viewed against other sources. Inevitably, when histories are written down long after the event, errors can genuinely occur. Where I have given dates, they are for guidance rather than a statement of absolute truth, and are based upon popular modern academic opinions.

Bretwalda

Much is made of who was the Bretwalda at any given period. The term seems to signify 'the senior or overlord king' but even that is open to debate. More importantly to my mind is that no academic has ever successfully explained how a king became one. Was it the one with the biggest army, most influence and wealth, or was it someone somehow democratically elected or acknowledged by the other kings? No one can say. There is even debate as to whether term was even recognised at the time, or was an invention of Bede or others. He and the Anglo Saxon Chronicle list some, but pointedly misses out the traditional enemies of his native Northumbria, the powerful Mercians such as Wulfhere, Æthelred or Æthelbald.

In the period covered by this book, the King of Kent, Æþelberht is succeeded by Raedwald of East Anglia in 616. When he dies in 625 it passes to Edwin of Deira, then on through Oswald of Northumbria (633) and Oswiu (642-70). What it meant in practice to be a Bretwalda is also uncertain: did other kings make gifts or give way on matters of national policy, or was it just an honorific title acknowledging who had got the most clout? We may never know for sure.

Abbreviations

To minimise the interference of references from the general flow of text I have used the following abbreviations:

ASC = Anglo Saxon Chronicle

BEH= Bedes Ecclesiastical History of the English Nation.

OE = Old English

Pronunciation

Old English pronunciation and translation is an in-exact art, subject to much debate. However, it can generally be agreed that

Þ,Ð, đ all equate to a 'th' sound.

Æ, æ equate to an 'ay' sound.

Beyond that it is open warfare!

Religion

Given that in the Pagan period, no Saxon became king without a claim to ancient lineage involving the god Woden or at least a tribal progenitor as an ancestor, conversion to Christianity presents them with a dilemma: should they add in some earlier ancestors going back to Noah or Adam and Eve, or is there another way of giving their dynasty the divine right to rule?

There becomes a new way of generating authority and respect: endow a church, monastery or similar and get one member of your family to run it. In these early days of Christianity, there is a reasonable chance they can be venerated as a saint after death, once more giving the dynasty a seal of approval from God. Maybe my interpretation is cynical, but it seems to be a recurring theme, with some figures being elevated into sainthood for fairly spurious reasons (such as dying in a battle against a Pagan or allowing missionaries into their kingdom) and being credited with miracles after death of healing and their body not decaying. In this book therefore may you forgive me if I do not always use the epithet saint for every royal personage after conversion to Christianity, and apologies to any genuine ones I malign in the process.

Later in the Anglo Saxon world there are even allegations of people setting up religious houses for their families to avoid taxes and military service whilst not conforming to any sort of monastic rules of living such as fasting, celibacy or not accruing wealth. It is no wonder that we find Penda's harsh attitude to religious hypocrites of any persuasion notable.

In this book I mainly use the generic term 'Heathen' to describe Penda's religious beliefs. It is derived from the Germanic term for a 'heath dweller' clinging to the old Pagan ideas, and was originally probably a derogatory term equivalent to 'country bumpkin.' Heathen essentially means the same as the Latin derived word Pagan (from pagani) meaning 'country dweller.' Both terms are collective nouns for a wide range of pre-Christian beliefs. Just as 'Christian' covers Catholic, Methodist, Baptist etc. so Heathen / Pagan collectively cover a number of spiritual paths.

Costume

Whilst we do not know for sure what Penda and his subjects wore, we do get an idea from archaeological finds and illustrated documents. There were many regional variations, probably related to the ethnic roots of the various tribal groups, be they Saxon, Jute or Frisian. Given that Penda fought a wide range of these, he may well have captured or been given as gifts items from cultures other than his own, such as the Welsh. Whether he then wore them to display his wide conquests, or kept a purer Mercian identity is impossible to know. There were also a succession of fashions, (some imported from abroad) initially slow to change but accelerated by the Christianisation of England, with its emphasis on simplicity, being humble etc. rather than the more exuberant Heathen styling's. It is quite probable that those proud of being Heathen made a point of proclaiming their identity: the manufacture and wearing of Thorshammer pendants seems to have increased in response the Christians display of crucifixes.

A high status male would most likely wear a linen shirt with a long woollen kirtle over it, hanging below the backside of woollen trousers. The neckline and cuffs may be decorated in braid, which protect them from fraying but also indicate higher status. The bottoms of the trousers may well have been bound with winingas, strips of material that strengthen and protect the ankles and trouser bottoms from mud and thorns. We have scant evidence on footwear, but simple leather turn shoes seem to have been worn by the better off.

Cuffs may be fastened with ornamented wrist clasps, and a woollen cloak secured by a large decorated annular, pen-annular or quoit pin brooch[4]. The leather belt was worn narrow, often with elaborate decorated metal buckle and strap end. On it, a seax knife would be worn to show one was a free man, and a purse. Separately on another broader belt a sword displayed status and power, and could be decorated with pyramid shaped cloisonné work. Penda is likely to have afforded complex gold and silver fittings and decoration for his scabbard and shield.

When going to war, a linen gambeson jacket padded with wool would protect his ribs from bruising and his clothing from damage by the iron mail armour worn over it. A substantial helmet is likely to have been worn by Penda to protect him in his many battles. His warriors (other than his elite housecarl bodyguards and rich followers) would have not had these advantages. A spear and shield is all the gear they were likely to be issued with.

Penda's wife Cyneswið may well have worn two bow or square headed brooches at her breasts to hold up a tubular

[4] (Hammond, 2009:25)

peplos type gown worn over a full length linen shift. They were in fashion in the area of Mercia during this period, although alternatives such as the cruciform brooch are also found in this area. As a wealthy woman she is likely to have had a costly necklace hung between the brooches, of amber, glass and wooden beads or semi- precious stones. She maybe had an extra brooch or two, either in bird or disc form. From her belt would be suspended a girdle hanger / chatelaine with household keys and toilet equipment such as tweezers, ear scoop and brush. Her fingers may have been adorned with a coiled or bezel gold ring. She may also have owned (and displayed) other high status belongings, such as a fine antler comb, glass drinking vessel or decorative spindle whorls for spinning.

Female hair was usually worn long up to the point of marriage, and then either cut or worn piled up under a scarf or hat. The coming of Christianity encouraged women to be more 'modest' and not reveal attractive hair or cleavage in low necklines.

Further down the social scale, just as now people liked to try and imitate the wealthier fashions, so rings may be manufactured from bone or wood, and brooches of base metals tinned to look like silver. Those at the very bottom may have had to rely on others cast-offs for clothes, and would not afford to have them dyed. It was possible if wealthy enough to obtain dyes of every colour at this time, apart from black. Some material would need dying several times over to get a darker shade, and some colours were difficult to fix. Red tended to fade in the light, so was rarely seen as a bright colour unless new.

Chapter 2

The origins of England, Mercia and Penda's Dynasty

The start of Anglo Saxon England is generally dated to around 450 CE, after the Romans had mainly abandoned Britain. However, it is not as clear cut as that: in the latter days of the decaying Roman Empire Saxon pirates raided across the sea, and so a chain of Saxon Shore Forts were built to repulse them. Some of their remains can still be seen at places such as Burgh on the river Waveney in Suffolk. The Romans also utilised many foreign troops in their occupation, and some of these may have been Germanic.

There has long been a passionate debate as to whether the Germanic tribes invaded by military force or simply migrated. Personally I think it was a combination of both: the native Celtic Britons were unlikely to have welcomed incomers with an invitation to take all the best land without armed resistance, but later generations of Germanic settlers would have been able to have taken advantage of the military gains of their forbears. Some Britons inevitably had to live alongside the invaders, but according to the mid 8th century writer Gildas, others fled to Wales or back to what we now call Gaul in France. It did not all go the right way for the Saxons though, and according to Nennius the Welsh recorded twelve victories against them, including a major conflict at Badon Hill in about 511 CE. Those defeats resulted in Angles & Frisians returning back across the sea to mainland Europe in around 550 (according to Procopius of Caesarea) losing some of the land they had previously gained.[5]

_____

[5] (Horn, 2011:15)

We also have the tale of a Celtic King Vortigen. 'Vortigen' may be interpreted as a 'King of Kings' title similar to the Saxon Bretwalda. The title may possibly have belonged to a Briton called Vitallinas. In any case the Welsh *Brut y Tywysogion* (Red Book of Herga) refers to 'Vortigen of Repulsive Lips', so the name did not naturally command respect maybe! He invited the Saxon brothers Hengist & Horsa to act as mercenaries to expel Picts and other tribes out of his kingdom in about 449. The story goes that having done that, they decided to settle, and rebelled against their employer at the battle of Ashingdon in Kent. The White Horse stone is said to commemorate the fall of Horsa there. That is a possibility, but the stone is thought to be part of a much older Neolithic chamber tomb. A second smaller stone is now buried under the road. Hengist survived to found a kingdom in the South East which gradually spread over most of modern day England. The name Hengist translates as 'stallion', whilst Horsa means 'horse.' I muse as to how likely it was for parents to name two brothers after the same animal. Were their names actually titles instead, just as Emperor Haille Selassie of Ethiopia was known as 'the Lion of Judah?'

Whatever the origins of Germanic incursions, we know that Angles, (of Angeln, Germany), the Saxons (from Lower Saxony and the Low Countries) Jutes (of the Jutland peninsular, Denmark), Frisians and possibly others settled various areas. The Frisians originally came from the coast of Belgium down to Southern Scandinavia, and revered Inguz, a form of Freyr as their main God. The Jutes were concentrated on the South coast around Kent. The Angles (who may have entered the country up to a century later according to some thinking) chose East Anglia (the North Folk & the South Folk) whilst the Frisians seem to have been spread throughout

Kent, East Anglia and Lincolnshire. Grave goods from the earliest Northumbrian sites appear similar to continental Frisian finds, so we may cautiously surmise that the origins of Mercia lie there, yet there was later much animosity between neighbouring Northumbria and Mercia, reflected in the way that Bede ignores or minimises their presence.. The name Mercia indicates in Old English 'Marches (Boundary) Folk.' The boundary between what would be the key question, and certainly its old boundaries appear to separate the Weolh (Welsh) from the rest of the Anglo Saxon world.

Stenton[6] states that 7th century Mercia was divided into North & South sub kingdoms divided by the river Trent, with the North having 7000 households and the South 5,000. One district south west of Birmingham was occupied by the Tomsætons (named after the river Tame). The Pecsætons occupied the Peak district of modern Derbyshire, centred on *Northworthy*, the modern Derby. To the South the Wreocensætons occupied the Wrekin area.

To the north of the upper Thames lay an area disputed by Mercia and Wessex. This was the land of the Hwicce, who gave their name to Wychwood Forest, which was much larger then. The Hwicce area and elsewhere have place names attributed to a Penda source: Pinbury in Gloucestershire, Pinvin and Pendiford both in Worcestershire, Penley in Flintshire and Peddimore in Warwickshire. There are also a scattering of place names thought to originate from his ancestors Pybba & Creoda.

Wood[7] adds to the list of tribes: the obscure Stoppingas of Wellesbourne, the Unecung-ga, the Noxgaga and the

[6] (Stenton, 2001:40-41)

Hendrica were all constituent tribes with individual ealdormen or sub kings, as well as the smaller Gile of the Ivel valley in modern Hertfordshire and the Hicce of Hitchin. A larger list of 34 constituent tribes is given in the Tribal Hidage, possibly drawn up by the administrators of King Offa or an earlier Mercian king.

This is a time of several kingdoms in a state of flux. It is sometimes referred to as the heptarchy, indicating seven, yet there were generally many more kingdoms, tribes and sub tribes jostling for position and power, as I indicate on the following maps of the situation in c.600 &.625:

---

[7] (Wood, 1981:86)

PICTS

DALRIADA

STRATHCLYDE

GODODDIN

BERNICIA

N. RHEGED

DEIRA

IOM.

S. RHEGED

ANGLESEY

ELMET

LINDSEY

GWYNEDD

POWYS

MERCIA

EAST ANGLES

DYFED

EAST SAXONS

WESSEX

SUSSEX

KENT

DUMNONIA

ISLE OF WIGHT

SKETCH MAP
OF ROUGH BOUNDARIES
IN 600 CE

SKETCH MAP
OF ROUGH
BOUNDARIES
IN 625 CE.

As you can see, there are large scale political changes in that 25 year period: The Bernician king Æthelfrith defeated a combined force of Dalriada Scots and Welsh Britons at *Catraeth* (Catterick) in 598. He later turned his attention on Deira but was stopped by Raedwald of East Anglia supporting

Edwin, the heir to that throne. Edwin ended up combining the kingdom of Deira jointly with that of Northumbria.[8] He was also overlord of the small kingdom of Lindsey, which he probably ruled via a local sub-king. William of Malmesbury states that when Raedwald died soon after this (c.624-5) that Edwin was accepted by the East Anglians as over king, with Raedwald's son Eorpwald as his local sub-king.[9]

Northumbria had absorbed or amalgamated the smaller kingdoms of Bernicia, Deira, Lindsey & Elmet and extended westwards to link to the Welsh border at Gwynedd & Powys and the West Coast of England to the north of them.

Raedwald of East Anglia inherited the kingdom from his father Tyttla in about 599, but did not become Bretwalda until 616 and the death of the previous one, King Æthelberht of Kent on the 24th February, whom he had visited.

King Æthelberht was said to be a direct descendant of Hengist, one of the original Saxon mercenary-settlers. His son Eadbald returned Kent to Paganism for a period and is accused by Bede of excessive fornication, including with his father's Queen, his stepmother according to Malmesbury and had fits of madness.

Meanwhile, still in 616 the Christian King Sabert of the East Saxons dies, and his three sons (Saeward, Seaxraed and Seaxbald) return their kingdom to Paganism, booting out the bishop to Kent when he refuses to give them communion bread. He said they should be baptised first, which they took

---

[8] (James & Fairbank, 1986: 14)
[9] (Malmesbury, 1989: 13)

exception to. Maybe they thought he was suggesting they needed a bath!

The Mercian dynasty is given as descending from Icel (probably the leader during the migratory period) then Creoda (or Cryda) c.585-593, Pybba (c.593-600) and Penda. Nennius says that Pybba had twelve sons, but only two of them are known by name: Penda and Eowa. (or Eawa) Because of their ancestor, the central Mercian tribe are sometimes referred to as the Iclingas, and claimed descent from the God Woden. Creoda's line is given as Woden -Wihtlaeg - Wermund – Offa – Angelþeow - Eomer – Icel-Creoda. It is a matter of speculation of what happened to the other ten un-named sons of Pybba? Did they support their brothers, or were they seen as a threat to be sent into exile or be assassinated?

Nennius gives an alternative expanded line of Woden- Guedolgeat – Gueagon – Guithleg – Guerdmond – Ossa – Ongen – Eamer – Pubba (Pybba). It is not possible to know within the genealogies of the period who are real ancestors and where some mythical figures are added or 'borrowed' from.

In 593 Creoda died in a battle with the Northumbrian king Ethelric, having reigned since about 586 in the early period of migration by the Angles. Ethelric also died, and Mercia was then ruled by Northumbria for a while under Æthelfrith, but he was eventually killed by Raedwald of East Anglia in 616, to be replaced by Edwin, who had been in exile at Raedwald's court.

The Iclingas already seem to have been dominant in the Midlands before Penda, based upon the Tribal Hidages list. This shows how many hides of land belonged to each tribal group. A hide is a flexible measurement, depending on the quality of the land for agriculture. One hide should be able to support one extended free family household, and could be singly ploughed in one year. An average hide size was about 120 acres, but could be much larger if the ground was not as easy to farm due to rocks, marsh etc. It was used as a way of calculating taxes due.

There is a strong possibility that Mercia was ruled by a pair of kings in the North and South at times, and Cearl (c.600-615) is a possible contender for this alongside Penda, followed by Eowa, the brother of Penda. It was not uncommon to have jointly ruled kingdoms at this time.

According to the Anglo Saxon Chronicle Penda did not become king until he was 50 years old, and reigned for 30 years. This would mean that he was about 73 when he led his final battle in 655 – unlikely but possible. E.g. Ealdorman Byrhtnoth was reckoned to be 60 when he fought the Danes at the Battle of Maldon.

> "The historian who appears to have most deeply considered the question of Penda's date of accession is Nicholas Brooks. He believes that the Chronicle entry for 626 was badly written. Rather than reading Penda held his kingdom for thirty years and he was fifty years old when he succeeded to the kingdom, Brooks believes that it would make more sense if it had originally said that Penda succeeded to the kingdom and reigned for thirty years, dying when he was fifty," [10]

---

[10] (Fox, 2008:15-21)

This would certainly fit in with his sons being of youthful age when he died, something one would not expect of an eighty year old, and would also accord with the age of his sister on marriage. For Penda to die at the age of 50 in 655 would fit reasonably comfortably with Bede (BEH) and the Welsh *Historica Brittonum*.[11]

Kingship was a dangerous business in those days, with the majority dying in battle or by assassination, or if lucky going into exile. It was also a world of shifting loyalties and politics, necessitating royal tours of progress around a country to reward friends and frighten enemies. Having a king and his courtly retinue come to visit was a costly honour, since the host would be expected to feed them all for the duration of the stay, whilst disputes were settled, land grants made and justice dispensed. A king may have a great hall (like the one found at Yeavering, Northumbria) but would only enjoy it for limited periods.

---

[11] (Brooks, 2000:70-73)

St. Nicholas Church, Littleborough, Notts., incorporating Roman bricks & Anglo Saxon pillars. Raedwald may have passed this way en route for the Battle of the River Idle. (below)

Chapter 3 The Battle of the River Idle, and Penda becomes King.

Æthelfrith of Bernicia was an experienced warrior, having beaten the Scots of Dalriada in 603 at the battle of Degastán. Æthelfrith had usurped Edwin; having got control of the kingdom of Deira in 604 by killing King Athelric. Iin 607, Aethelfrith invaded Gwynedd to get to Edwin but was challenged by a combined Briton force at Chester. They were beaten by Aethelfrith, and King Iago and King Selyf Sarffgadau of Powys were killed. Another king Brocmail survived and fled with the survivors. Aethelfrith's quest to subdue Wales and kill Edwin continues in 613 at the Battle of Bangor-is-Coed. This time King Bledric of Dumnonia is killed along with a thousand monks praying for his victory and Aethelfrith takes control of South Rheged and marries Acha of Deira in about 615. She was the daughter of King Aelle. How willing she was to marry Aethelfrith, with him being responsible for the death of her father we do not know.

Her wily (or lucky) brother Edwin fled to take refuge at the court of King Iago in Gwynedd, and then escaped once more to seek refuge with King Raedwald of East Anglia. Cwenburga of Mercia became married to Edwin. Why someone would marry off his daughter to a man in exile, with few prospects and a target for assassination by Aethelfrith is curious. It was only the fact that Raedwald decided to help his refugee Edwin by fighting at the Battle of the River Idle the next year in 616 that improved his prospects.

According to the ASC, in about 626 Penda became King of Mercia. He was the son of Pybba & Pyt, The exact date and circumstances are uncertain: Cearl is also written about as a

Mercian king at this time, so Penda may have been a successor related by family or a rival in that the kingdom may have been ruled in two halves by two kings – not unique at the time. Stenton[12] suggests that he was initially a landless warrior thegn. His combined kingdom has become known as Southumbria, and was about half the size of Northumbria, and if he was a joint king then he was probably the southernmost with Cearl in the north.

Penda's queen was Cyneswið, the sister of Cynegils who bore him seven children: three sons (Peada, Wulfhere & Æþelræd) and four daughters (Merewalh, Cyneburh, Cyneswith & Wilburga). Cynegils was one of the kings of Wessex that Penda defeated at Cirencester, so it is possible that his sister Cyneswið was married to him as part of the peace treaty terms. She was later trusted to keep Ecgfrith, the 10 year old hostage son of Oswiu captive whilst her husband was at war. Cynegils was converted to Christianity by the Lombard St. Berin (Bishop Birinus) in about 636 and as a result apparently King Oswald of Northumbria offered him an alliance plus his acceptance of Cynegils daughter for a wife.[13] Berin was supported to make his headquarters at Dorchester.

Newton[14] argues that Penda was effectively the Bretwalda i.e. 'Ruler of Britain' from after the death of King Æthelfrith of Northumbria at the Battle of the River Idle on 24th February, 616.

King Raedwald of the Wuffing dynasty of East Anglia had fought alongside his son Reginhere and Edwin whom he had

---

[12] (Stenton, 2001)

[13] (Horswell, 1985: 71)

[14] (Newton, 2003)

sheltered as an exile from Northumbria. Bribes had been offered by Æthelfrith of Bernicia to surrender Edwin, but Raedwald had been persuaded by his wife to protect his guest. As well as King Æthelfrith, Reginhere died also.

This battle between the principal forces of North and South is believed to have been fought at Eaton, on the southern edge of modern East Retford, (on the Western boundary of the kingdom of Lindsey) well into the enemies territory. Æthelfrith had his back to the bank of the River Idle, possibly using an old Roman fort with three ditch defences to make up for a seeming tactical disadvantage. Apparently the fort was already decayed, like the one referred to in the OE poem 'The Ruin.' [15]

If Raedwald was advancing from the Littleborough direction (as suggested by Newton) he may have travelled by ship up through the Humber estuary then South on the River Trent using the navigable rivers inland until he reached Littleborough, the old Roman site of *Segilocum*. A principally Norman church there, the tiny St. Nicholas includes Roman bricks and Anglo Saxon pillars. The church was not recorded in the Domesday Book, but is believed to have incorporated earlier Roman & Saxon sites. The later building could have been commissioned by the Norman William the Bastard (the Conqueror) since it lay in his personal manor of Mansfield. Originally the rivers ran differently, before being diverted to their present courses, and there is not a direct link there today between the Trent and Idle rivers.

From Littleborough it is only about 8 miles further west to Eaton, which could have been marched quickly or even

[15] (Alexander: 1977: 28)

reached by connecting up further South on the Trent with the River Idle at Stockwith, providing it was navigable. The area seems to have been an important one in Saxon times with a mint and potteries being established at Torksey (nowadays part of nearby Retford) by the 10th century. It was formerly the Roman settlement of *Tiovulfingacester* and Bishop Paulinus baptised many people there in front of King Edwin of Northumbria.

The River Idle also runs parallel to a section of the old Roman Ermine Street road from York to London, so one could theorise that the old Roman fort site was at a point that could control both the road and any river crossing, which would still be relevant centuries later for Æthelfrith.

River Idle

The Welsh Triads 10 and 32[16] give an account of the battle, which includes the presence of Welsh forces fighting on

Raedwald's side. A Chieftain named as Sganfell, the son of Dissynyndawd is named as the slayer of Æthelfrith.[17] Presumably the Welsh had their own grievances to settle and took the opportunity to merge with a larger force to help resolve them.

Unlike many other comparatively short battles of the period, this one was described as long, and a saying supposedly originated from it: "The River Idle was foul with the blood of Englishmen." (From Amnia Idle Anglorum sanguine sordit: The blood of the Angles stains the river of Idle. *Trans. Georius*)

Henry of Huntingdon[18] claimed that the East Anglian army was split into three units, led by Reginhere, Edwin & Raedwald. Reginhere was possibly mistaken for Raedwald, and targeted by his enemy in a cutting out operation. Then Raedwald broke from his own lines to seek out and kill Æthelfrith personally, so there is dispute as to who had the honour. Afterwards, when Raedwald helped Edwin to take over Northumberland, the old king Æthelfrith's sons were sent into exile.

Reginhere being mistaken for his father might not be so far-fetched: Raedwald's distinctive masked helmet (since reconstructed) and fabulous buckle, purse, shoulder clasps and shield fittings have long been admired since their excavation in the 1930s at Sutton Hoo. A fragment of another helmet was found with a broken section of decoration very similar to it in the area where the battle was fought. Could it be that two were made, one for the king, and one for his son the atheling Prince? Personally I tend to think not: the fragment

---

[16] (Bromwich, 1961)
[17] (Goch, 1425)
[18] (Greenway, 1977)

was from a high status 7th century burial mound at Caenby, which is about 28 miles from Eaton. Unless Reginhere died from his wounds on the way back from the battle, I would think he would either be buried at the battlefield, or taken all the way back to the royal burial ground at Sutton Hoo, and not buried elsewhere without good reason, such as it being an existing burial site for that kingdom.

Sutton Hoo burial mounds, Suffolk.

It does of course beg the question who else may have owned the helmet? Caenby is near the border lands of the old Elmet and Lindsey kingdoms, so it could be royalty from either place. Given that Raedwald had passed through the kingdoms without problems, it would appear that they were either tacitly or actively supporting him, and could have endured loss alongside him, although no mention is made of this in the remaining records.

Both Raedwald & Reginhere are also have been likely to have worn high status clothing and armour associated with their rank: a sword, mail armour over a padded gambeson jacket, ornamented shield and brightly coloured clothing made of dyed linen or wool, with expensive jewelled buckles and brooches & pins, and be surrounded by housecarl bodyguards..

After the death of Raedwald in 624, another son Eorpwald (who converted to Christianity influenced by King Edwin of Northumberland in 627) inherited the Anglian crown, but was usurped by a third brother Ricbert (a Pagan) who reigned from 627-30 until Sigeberht, (a Christian returned from exile in France) took his place from 630-640. He re-Christianised the area with the help of St. Felix.

As you can see, there was a fluctuation of faith in East Anglia at this period. King Raedwald was a Pagan when he visited Æþelberht the Bretwalda King of Kent, who had been Christianised by his wife Berhte of Paris. He was unwilling to do business with Raedwald as a Pagan, and persuaded him to be baptised. Sending him home with priests and presents, (probably including the Saulus & Paulus Apostle spoons found in his burial), he would have been disappointed to know that his supposed new convert placed the cross on an altar alongside his other Pagan ones in his temple at Rendlesham. Maybe in a time of mixed religions he thought he should acknowledge all the ones being followed by his people. However, his un-named wife remained Pagan and saw to it that he had the most spectacular Pagan ship burial of Mound 1, Sutton Hoo.

There are no contemporary pictures of Penda, and as far as we know no coins were minted in his name. (The window from Durham cathedral is speculative of what he looked like and created long after he died.) Most trade at the time was bartered, and currency requires a stable regime for people to trust its' continued value. We can surmise that when he became rich from the spoils of battle and the income from his lands that he would have invested some wealth into having fine clothes, jewellery, armour and horses like other 7th century leaders of the time at Sutton Hoo, Suffolk, Prittlewell & Broomfield in Essex and Taplow in Buckinghamshire. (Tæppa of Taplow was possibly of 7th century Kentish origins based on the artefacts found, and was buried on the boundary of several kingdoms in an area overrun by Penda, and thus may have been a sub king.)

Fine armour, clothing and jewellery would not be a simple case of vanity, but a way of impressing his subjects and enemies of his high standing. At that time if you had wealth you flaunted it as a badge of your status, and if you examine museum exhibits of the period you will soon realise that rather than being the 'Dark Ages' it was a period of exquisite craftsmanship and vibrant, colourful artistry. To some modern eyes some artefacts may seem gaudy, but do not forget that lighting levels were low in the buildings of this period, and the costly ornamentation was designed to be seen by the flickering hearth fire, beeswax candles and tallow rush lights, with textured gold foils reflecting light through the impossibly minute cloisonné cells of the items in the shadowy gloom.

Reconstructed Anglo Saxon house, West Stow, Suffolk.

Accommodation

Ordinary houses tended to be rectangular and thatched, with a single door, central hearth fire and possibly shuttered windows. Some had a second storey, and others had a sunken floor beneath floorboards known as *grubenhaus*. This would have provided a dry drained floor with space underneath for storage. Walls were often daub and wattle i.e. clay / dung pressed into woven stick frames, particularly where there was no building stone available. However, large timber clad halls (such as Yeavering) were also constructed.

Generally, there wasn't a chimney in the thatched roof, so smoke from the hearth fire slowly seeped through it, smoking meat and fish hung in the rafters. Some buildings may have had apertures at the end of the roof or over a door to allow smoke to disperse, but in my re-enactor practical experiences at the reconstructed Anglo Saxon houses of West Stow in Suffolk it does not seem to be a major problem.

There would have likely to have been some store and craft working buildings, plus a larger hall for the leader to act as a communal gathering place and home for the leader, his family, guests and possibly servants / slaves.

There were few substantial towns in the 7th century, with most people living in extended family homesteads or villages of maybe a few dozen families. Larger settlements tended to be based around more intensive work activities such as pottery, trading markets, shipbuilding or metal working. Later settlements grew from supporting communities for a palace or monastery. Armies on the move did use some tents to shelter in if buildings were unavailable or insufficient for their needs.

Social classes and food

However, a king was expected to circulate around his people, to judge legal cases, set new laws and collect tribute or taxes, institute new projects, reward friends and exert power over less loyal subjects. It also had the effect of lessening the burden to his own resources in that his hosts (mainly *ealdormen* who ruled districts on the King's behalf) were expected to provide him and his court with food and lodging. He would be accompanied by his counsellors *(witan)* any *atheling* princes, his bodyguards *(housecarls)* and some of the younger aristocracy *(thegns)* hoping to make a name for themselves (mainly through military prowess), as well as personal servants, keepers of hawks and hounds etc. Below the *thegns* were the *ceorls*, mainly free peasant farmers. Bottom of the social scale were *đeow*, the slaves and bondsmen. Providing a feast for followers is an important component in spreading a sense of wellbeing and loyalty, and Penda would have been judged on his generosity, who he gave honoured places, what entertainment was provided (such as a storyteller or musician) and the amount of mead, ale or even wine consumed.

It is likely that King Penda would have only been called upon to judge complex legal cases that could not be settled at the local thing, a form of parish council and court combined. There is no evidence of written laws for Penda, although he may have had some. More likely is that some trusted men would be able to recite the traditional laws from memory, and counsellors help guide the king in interpreting them. There were some written law codes in existence at the time, from continental Germanic sources and nearer to home from Æþelberht of Kent in about 602.[19] This code was based on those of the Franks and others and carried levels of wergild (compensation) for a variety of injuries and crimes as well as spelling out the relationship between the early church with the King.

Of course it was the lower classes that produced most of the food by farming or fishing, although theoretically anyone could go gathering wild fruit and nuts or hunting at the time. (Hunting laws were later restrictions imposed by the Normans.) The diet was healthy and varied for those who could afford it: bread was the staple, potatoes not being available at the time, but versions of most other modern English fruit and vegetables were cultivated, providing basic vegetable stews augmented by meat occasionally. Many of the crops would

---

[19] (Griffiths, 1998: 24)

have been much smaller than today: plant development has since produced larger vegetables that give bigger, pest resistant crops. It has been estimated that barley crops have increased ten-fold for the same field size from then until the present day.

Cows were kept mainly for their dairy products but pigs could provide piglets for eating regularly. A sheep's value was in its wool, with weaving woollen cloth being the main way of creating a surplus to trade with and export in exchange for other goods not locally available. (Linen was also available to weave into clothes.) Some food could be preserved for use in winter, such as dried peas and beans and smoked meat and fish, but famines following a bad harvest were not uncommon. There was also the possibility of gathering seasonal berries, fruits, nuts and herbs to augment and vary the menu.

Whilst some cooking was done in a pot directly over a fire, there is good evidence that an indirect method was often used: heating a stone in a fire that was then transferred to the cooking pot.[20]

Slavery

Wealthy leaders would have employed a number of slaves, and they constitute about 10% of the workforce at this time. Half a pound of silver seems to be the average going rate for an adult male slave, equivalent to about £30,000 at today's rates and at the same time around the same price as for a horse. The Old English word Weolh has a dual meaning: 'Welsh' and 'slave', giving a good indication of where many slaves originated from. Welsh in this context probably included

---

[20] (Hagen, 92: 47)

foreign prisoners of war from the indigenous Briton occupation as well as Celts and Picts.

There were two other ways of becoming a slave: if one committed a crime and could not raise the fine or *wergild* (damages) one possibility was for the *thing* (council-cum-court) to give a sentence of slavery instead. The other was if a family became destitute members may be offered to a local lord for free in exchange for keeping them in food, clothes and shelter, rather than that they starve to death.

There were ways for slaves to become free: they may be given freedom for exceptional service e.g. saving a life or buy it by working for themselves on their permitted day off. On conversion to Christianity, some Saxon slave owners gave slaves freedom, (known as manumission) but this was often postponed until their death. Both Heathens and Christians had specific ceremonies for freeing slaves in front of witnesses.

There were various other laws relating to slaves, penalising a master for getting a female servant pregnant (if she could prove paternity of course) and damages payable to the owner of a slave that was injured or killed.[21] One of the effects of Christianity was to make slaves worse off: the church insisted that slaves should attend services on Sunday, and should be beaten by their masters if they refused. This meant that slaves had less free time to work on their own account to make personal wealth which they may have one day used to buy their freedom. The king had a financial

---

[21] (Pelteret, D., 1995)

interest in slavery, generally getting a 4 pence tax on each one, and slavery was not outlawed until the reign of Cnut.

Chapter 4

The Welsh and West Saxons Rebel

Since the Battle of Dyrham in 577 the Welsh had been isolated from their fellow Celts in Dumnonia That kingdom was in the area of Devon and Somerset, and at that time appears to have been separate to the neighbouring Cornovii of modern Cornwall. There were a series of raids by Saxons into Wales including one in 615 resulting in the slaughter of many monks at Bangor. One wonders whether this is the same attack mentioned in ASC:

> This year Cynegils and Cwichelm fought at Beandun and slew two thousand and forty six of the Welsh. (ASC)

It has been thought that Beandun was possibly Bindon, near Axmouth in Devon, and that their chief opponent was King Clemen, and that he withdrew with a badly mauled army to Exeter (Caer-Uisc).

Thirteen years later in 628 King Cyneglis of Wessex and his relation (possibly son) King Cwichelm of the Gewisse tribe fought Penda at Cirencester. There does not seem to be a clear reason given for the battle. Maybe it was simply a territorial dispute between the two neighbouring kingdoms of Mercia and Wessex.

Penda must have done well with his Iclingas war band because a treaty ceded Cirencester and an area of the river Severn to Penda. The sub kingdom of the Hwicce tribe of the modern Worcestershire, Gloucestershire & West Warwickshire seems to have been created then, so it may be conjectured that the tribe were his allies.

The ASC states that in 636:

> This year King Cwichelm was baptised at Dorchester, and died the same year." (ASC)

That means that Cwichelm was still a fellow Pagan when he fought Penda in 628. Cynegils was baptised at the same time, meaning that he also was initially Pagan. They were baptised by Bishop Birinus, and Oswald of Bernicia acted as his Godfather.

> This year [648] Cenwalh gave his relation Cuthred three thousand hides of land by Ashdown. Cuthred was the son of Cwichelm, Cwichelm of Cynegils. (ASC)

It has been thought that Cuthred may have been a sub king under Cynegils and Cenwalh. The actual relationship between Cwichelm and Cyneglis is a disputed one, reliant on the nuances of translation. Cyneglis had come to power in 611 after the death of King Ceolwulf.

A further complication is that Edwin married Cwenburga, widow of the north Mercian king Ceorl who is thought to have died in 615. One wonders whether it was an attempt by Edwin to gain advantage over, and make an ally of North Mercia. It would have benefited Edwin to prevent her from marrying Penda to unite north and south Mercia. We may deduce that Eowa took over in North Mercia at this time, preventing Penda from being able to seize control of the whole of Mercia.

Edwin went on to conquer North Rheged in Wales, Ynys Manau (Isle of Man) and Elmet, killing King Ceretic. This all happened in around 617. Three years later in 620 he retakes South Rheged (which had rebelled) and King Llywarch fled to Gwynedd which is still free. Edwin went on to move North, attacking Southern Strathclyde and Gododdin. With this catalogue of war on so many fronts, it seems rather unfair that Penda is solely credited with being the warlike one, but Bede was always going to favour a Christian of Northumbria over a Pagan of Mercia.

There was an assassination attempt on Edwin by a West Saxon at the River Derwent on Easter Day 626, allegedly ordered by Cwichelm according to Bede. The ASC concurs, naming the assassin as Eumer, who tried to assassinate Edwin with a 'two-edged dagger, dipped in poison.' The fact that the weapon is so described maybe hints that it was of an unusual form: the usual shape for a hand knife was a one edged seax, with a sloping end rather than a pointed tip. The king was partly saved by Lilla, a member of his court who threw himself in the way. Another defender Forthhere was also killed. Continuing the drama Edwin's Queen Cwenburh (or Ethelburga) gave birth to a daughter called Eanfled the same night. It must have been quite a day!

Edwin sought divine assistance from Bishop Paulinus. Having routed the West Saxons in revenge he eventually converted to Christianity from Paganism. The competing religious currents can clearly be still seen on the Northumbrian early 8th century whalebone casket, with its scenes of both Christian and Pagan mythology, and accompanying runic script. It is known as the Franks casket (after its modern owner) and can be seen at the British Museum.

When he was debating whether to convert in around 627, one of his advisors told a parable of a sparrow flying out of foul weather into a warm hall, but who carried on out of the hall back into the dark winter weather. The advisor said it was like the life of a man: what went before or after was uncertain.[22]

His chief Heathen priest Coifi offered to set an example to the people by profaning the temples. He was given arms and a stallion to ride (both taboo acts for a priest) and went to cast a spear into the Heathen temple at Godmundingham, (now Goodmanham, E Yorkshire) smashed the idols and set fire to it.

Returning to Wales, King Edwin of Northumbria landed a force on a Welsh island, Yns Mon, (Anglesey) in 633, but was unable to cross the Menai Straits. Bede says Edwin was always preceded in peace as well as war by a banner, in the manner of the Romans *tufa*. *Tufa* is a term that can include a tuft of hair or feathers being used as a flag, as in a Roman helmet crest.

The Saxon threat to Wales had eventually prompted King Cadwallon ap Cadfan of Gwynedd to retaliate. Cadwallon suffered several defeats to his forces by Edwin's army, and being trapped on the Isle of Priestholm (Ynys Lannog) escaped to Ireland, then on to Guernsey and Brittany. A Welsh source suggests that Edwin was originally the foster-uncle of Cadwallon, giving a personal edge to the conflict.

On his return to Britain via the South Coast to retake his kingdom, he got caught up with a Mercian siege of Exeter. It had been the Briton King Clemens bolt hole back in 615, and

---

[22] (Alexander, 1977: 64)

although we cannot be sure, he may still have been in charge there at the time. Cadwallon defeated Penda, but then formed an alliance with him against King Edwin of Northumbria. It was sealed by Cadwallon marrying Penda's sister Alcfrith. Maybe with the view that my enemies' enemy is my friend, Penda quite willingly joined the Welsh king with his own war band. Anyway, he assisted his new ally to regain Gwynedd at the Battle of Cefn Digoll (Long Mountain, near Welshpool.)

Bede says Cadwallon was supported vigorously by Penda, who afterwards reigned in Mercia for 22 years. It is likely that the Yeavering Hall complex (a powerbase for Edwin in Bernicia) was burnt during this rampage in about 632. (Laing, 1979: 156) The site can be visited, and a hall has been reconstructed in pictures for the modern visitor to see on the Gefrin Trust[23] website as well as a video about the excavations.

Edwin died at the age of 47 on 12th October 633 at the battle of Haethfelth/ Heavensfield (called by Welsh sources the Battle of Meigan and more recently identified as Hatfield Chase near Doncaster) together with his son Osfrid, and his army was destroyed or dispersed. Conversely Thatcher and others have challenged the site,[24] suggesting a Northumbrian alternative.

---

[23] (Gefrin Trust, 2011)
[24] (Griffiths, 1992:18-19)

Hatfield Chase – probable site of Battle of Haethfelth, Yorkshire.

Apparently Edwin had a palace (or somewhat more likely a hunting lodge) at Hatfield, thought to be on the site of the more recent manor house. He had also built a church there[25] It is thought that Edwin formed his troops up on some high ground nearby, close to the south bank of the river Don. Some higher ground has been identified at the back of the present manor estate.

After the battle Northumbria collapsed as a state. Cadwallon ap Cadfan of Gwynedd claimed the crown of Deira. The kingdom was then split between Deira and Bernicia, under Osric, a cousin of Edwin.

If as thought Bede measured the start of a new year from September, one can suspect that Penda became king of the

[25] (Tomlinson, 1882:32)

wider kingdom in about 632. He ravaged Northumbria with Cadwallon for about a year, burning York and sacking Yeavering, before heading southwards.

Meanwhile, Osric of Northumberland challenged Cadwallon at York, later in 633, but was defeated. The Pagan King Eanfrith of Bernicia (Aethelfrith's son who had been in exile under Edwin) tried to negotiate peace but was killed by people loyal to Oswald. Then this half brother Oswald returned from exile in the Scots kingdom of Dalriada, and defeated and killed Cadwallon at the Battle of the Wall (or Denisesburn), near Hexham in 635.according to Welsh sources. Although the Annals of Wales (*Annales Cambriae*) stated it as:

> *631 The battle of Cantscaul in which Cadwallon fell.*

A song is recorded in Latin by Henry of Huntingdon about the battle, here translated by Georius:

> *Caedes Cadwalensium Denisi cursus coercuit:*

> *The killing of Cadwalla at Denises prevented the flight (with horses?).*

Cadwallan had marched North up the old Dere Street Roman road, and they were exhausted by the time they reached Oswald's position. Oswald had erected a cross and got his men to pray, so it is thought that they had plenty of time to prepare and rest. They chased the Welsh back south, with Cadwallan reportedly being killed at Rowley Burn.

Marsden[26] (makes a case for the Irish settlement of Scotic Dalriada sending a war band to help Oswald, in return for his

[26] (Marsden,1992:28)

fighting for them in Irish dynastic wars as a young man in exile. He was also accompanied by a contingent of monks from Iona. His contact with the latter (and continuing friendship with St. Cuthbert) may well have influenced him toward a Celtic brand of Christianity, rather than the Roman model he inherited in Northumbria. Whilst in power he extended the Northumbrian grip on the small independent kingdom of Lindsey from his base in Bernicia.

After the withdrawal of Penda, Oswald went on to rule the whole of a once more united Northumbria. He also expanded his kingdom northwards into Scotland, capturing Edinburgh, headquarters of the Briton Gododdin tribe, plus the Lothian area. With a major ally Cadwallon killed, Penda must have felt at a disadvantage. He would still have been establishing his power, organisation and calculating who he could count on as a friend. Although one of Edwin's sons Osfrith died before his father, another one called Eadfrith had gone over to King Penda after the deaths. Penda had him killed in the reign of Oswald, apparently contrary to an oath he made to him. With Eadfrith as a potential inheritor of the kingship of Northumbria (or at least a sympathiser of Oswald), and the son of a king he had killed, it is little wonder that Penda may have suspected his allegiance.

The Staffordshire Hoard at Tamworth.

The recent exciting find of the Staffordshire Hoard at Tamworth has caused a lot of speculation, and when the lengthy conservation work has been completed it will undoubtedly challenge some previously held ideas about the period. So far, the huge collection of sword hilts (with their blades chopped away) has almost doubled the total number excavated from this period overnight. There is a total of about 5kg of gold and 2.5kg of silver in the 3,500 piece find.[27] With them are three gold pectoral crosses, (probably originally mounted on wood) their arms folded roughly to make them smaller. One is inscribed with a biblical text from Numbers, 10.35 to bring victory over ones enemies. *"Rise up O Lord, and may thy enemies be dispersed and those who hate thee be driven from thy face."*

That folding action hardly seems what one would expect from a Christian victor (which would exclude several other northern local kings of the time.): The tentative dating of the hoard is 650-750. Could it possibly be the spoils of one of Penda's victories? It is certainly within his home area, and of roughly the right period. The Anglo Saxon metal specialist Leahy[28] is quoted in the Guardian:

> Leahy said he was not surprised at the find being in Staffordshire, the heartland of the "militarily aggressive and expansionist" 7th century kings of Mercia including Penda, Wulfhere and Æthelred. "This material could have been collected by any of these during their wars with Northumbria and East Anglia, or by someone

[27] (Wilcox, 2011)
[28] (Kennedy, 2009)

whose name is lost to history. Here we are seeing history confirmed before our eyes."

Sword blades at that time were mainly made of iron with added carbon, (steel) but some of poorer quality were easily bent or chipped in battle. Reliably refined steel was not perfected for another century or two in some locations, and few had the luxury of an extremely expensive pattern welded sword.

It made sense to separate the precious metals and jewels of the hilts from the blades before recycling. Suggestions that this may have been a smith's scrap heap are laughable, unless smiths were as wealthy as kings in those days! One also has to remember that a sword was still a prestige weapon of status: the majority of Saxon warriors were armed simply with a shield and one or two spears, and little armour. It has been estimated that in the 7th century maybe only one warrior in 1-200 possessed a sword, and even then some would have been family heirlooms rather than new weapons. Although of very slightly lower quality work than the Sutton Hoo relics, these are substantial high status finds. I would therefore favour a more northern kingdom than East Anglia for their origin, and initial expert opinion has suggested that by their style they are more likely to come from the north, such as Northumbria.

The noted historian Michael Wood is reported as saying he believed that the Staffordshire Treasure Hoard had formed part of an enormous payment given to Penda by Oswald when he agreed to lift a siege of his forces in 654 at Stirling. (Oswald had taken Edinburgh in 638.) With the treasure dating to around 650 (some say a few years after that) and many pieces believed to be of Northumbrian design, Wood suggests that it was buried by the Mercians (which by then would have been under the command of Peada) before they were attacked by a Welsh army in 655 at Wall.[29]

The fact that the treasure contains lots of sword hilts, with the blades hacked off is an interesting one: If it was given as payment to lift a siege, the enemy would probably be reluctant to give their victors whole weapons

The fact that Christian crosses have been folded up also suggests that they were not valued as religious objects by their new owner, which may lead to the conclusion that the depositor of the hoard was Heathen. Although Penda would have been the new Pagan owner, his successor Peada was a Christian, so it may exclude him as the desecrator of the crosses. The contributing factor is that of the hoards alleged Northumbrian source: Oswald of Bernicia was most likely to have sourced his weapons there.

---

[29] (Howells & Leonard, 2010:25)

Chapter 5 The Battle of Maserfelth & 7th century warfare

On 5th August, 642, Penda was able to take on and defeat Oswald of Northumbria at the Battle of Maserfelth (possibly Oswestry from Oswald's Tree), Shropshire, which at the time was held as Welsh Powys territory. (Alternative views place it as Mackerfield, midway between Wigan and Warrington.) In any case, Penda was supported by Welsh allies (who if it were at Oswestry were fighting against an invader on their home territory.) They included (according to the Welsh tragic poetry of *Marwnad Cynddylan*) Cynddylan ap Cyndrwyn of Powys, of whom it was said:

> "When the son of Pyd (Pybba) requested, how ready he was." [30]

It is also believed that troops were provided from Gwynedd.

It was probably a combination of revenge for killing his ally Cadwallon, and a chance to weaken the threat to Mercia from an increasingly powerful Northumbria. Penda's brother Eowa died fighting on his side in the battle, probably indicating that he had been supporting Penda.[31] The verse below indicates he was a king, either supporting the theory of a dual kingship for North and South Mercia or that alternatively Penda succeeded him as sole king. A third possibility is that he was fighting on Oswald's side as a sub-king ally – the text does not indicate which is true.

Oswald's head and limbs were stuck on wooden stakes, maybe as a deterrent to other foes and in fury for killing his

---

[30] (Clancy, 1970)

[31] (Plunkett, 2005:109)

friend Cadwallon. Personally I do not support the discredited Margaret Murray orientated view of ritualistic killing and mutilation supported by Stone[32] but the theory that this was a Pagan reproducing the Norse myth of Ymir being ritually dismembered to create the universe is an entertaining one. As far as I know Ymir has never been identified in an Anglo Saxon context, although the mythology has the same Germanic origins.

A shrine to Oswald was erected in St. Peters Church, Bamburgh (somewhere under where the castle now stands) but Oswald's head was eventually laid in his friend St. Cuthbert's tomb at Durham Cathedral, having been moved from an interim site at Lindisfarne by Oswiu. His arm ended up at Medehamsted (Peterborough) where a chapel was built for it, complete with a sentry post for a monk to guard it from further theft. They had good reason, since they had stolen it from Bamburgh. Oswald became revered as a saint across Europe.

---

[32] (Stone, 2011)

St. Oswald's chapel, Peterborough Cathedral, Cambridgeshire.

The *Annales Cambriae* called Maserfelth the Battle of Cogfry.

> *644 The battle of Cogfry in which Oswald king of the Northmen and Eawa king of the Mercians fell.*[33]

The religious nature of the battle is reflected in the song written down in Latin by Henry of Huntingdon:

Campus Maserfeld sanctorum canduit ossibus:

The field of Maserfeld glowed (white) with the bones of the saints.

---

[33] (Annales Cambriae trans. J. Ingram, 1912)

St. Oswald banner, Lincoln cathedral.

The battle had the desired effect, because Oswald was succeeded by two rival kings who split Northumbria back into two of its constituent kingdoms: His brother Oswiu, who was 30 years old, ruled Bernicia in the North East to the north of the river Tees whilst Oswine controlled Deira, part of modern North Yorkshire.

With Eawa his co-king dead, Penda was not one to rest on his laurels. He also captured other parts of Deira in 643, as well as parts of Lincolnshire and the small kingdom of Elmet, which he placed under the control of Edwin's grandson Osric.

Oswine had been in exile on the Scottish island of Iona during Edwin's reign. On coming to power in Deira, he stayed Pagan for a while. However, after winning a battle against the Welsh at the Battle of Heavenfield at Chollerford north of Hexham in 635, he erected a cross on the site and converted to Christianity. He had led his men in Christian prayers before the battle, and brought in an Irish monk he had met on Iona called Aidan to be his bishop. Aidan chose Lindisfarne as his centre of operations.

A stone cross beside the B6318 east of Chollerford (close to the Roman Wall) marks the battlefield, with a church to the North marking where Oswine made his stand.

As Tyler points out:

> Penda raided Bernicia several times while Oswine was ruling the Deiri, and his line of march would have taken him through the territory of that people, yet we hear of no strife between the two kings, nor of Penda wasting and plundering here in the way he did further north. Thus it is possible that Oswine was subject to Penda's *imperium*; at the very least he was benevolently neutral and prepared to allow Penda and his forces to repeatedly traverse his lands.[34]

The agreement to split the constituent kingdoms of Northumberland between the two brothers did not last: in 651 Oswiu of Bernicia challenged Oswine of Deira at Wilfars Hill, Catterick. Oswine backed down without a battle, as he was

[34] (Tyler, 2005:8)

heavily outnumbered, and went into hiding at the Gilling home of Earl Hunwald with a single follower called Tonhere. He and his companion were however betrayed by the Earl and killed by one of Oswiu's commanders called Ethilyn on 20th August, 651.

Oswiu then seized Deira, citing his marriage to the daughter of King Edwin, Eanfled as the justification. He set up Ethelwald, a son of Oswald as his subordinate king in Deira in about 651. Ethelwald appears not to have done all that his benefactor wanted though, as the next year in 652 he joined forces with Penda!

7th Century Warfare

Whilst we may blithely dismiss battles of this period as 'A' beat 'B' the reality of the combat is complex and bloody. We have few details of tactics and dispositions, and even troop strengths when given are suspect since the victors may exaggerate their accomplishment by changing the size of their enemy in their accounts.

The basic Anglo Saxon warrior was armed with one or two spears plus a shield, and little else. The spears may be short javelin spears for throwing, and include *angons. Angons* bend on impact to make them difficult to extract from a shield, thus making it unwieldy to use. They also had barbs making them difficult to pull out and a long metal shaft end to prevent it being cut off near the point. One excavated at Abingdon, Oxfordshire had a metal end over 20 inches long in total. The favoured wood for spear shafts was ash, although other timber may have been used at times.

Longer spears (around 7 foot/ 2 metres long) were used to thrust from the line of the shield wall. The shields themselves were ideally made of linden (lime) wood which is close grained yet light, but of surviving fragments it seems that up to half of them were made of other woods. Shields were generally round, made of three or four planks glued together, with a hide or metal rim reinforcement. The centre was covered in a conical metal boss that absorbed the worst of blows as well as protecting the hand gripping the crossbar strengthening the back of the shield. The shield boss could also be used offensively: smashing it into the opponents face. One can also use the shield with the whole body behind it to barge into an opponent to unbalance them. Some 6-7th century shield bosses had a button mounted on the cone, which tends to disrupt and catch the opponent's weapon, but they seem to have fallen out of use by the 8th century.

Although there are isolated incidents of forces using cavalry[35] in general higher status men with horses would dismount and fight on foot, forming part of the shield wall at the start of a battle. However, William of Malmesbury cites Angles pursuing retreating Scots with cavalry in the very earliest period they were in Britain.[36] Warriors would most usually stand shoulder to shoulder in a line, overlapping shields, with spears protruding between them. Obviously this tactic is only as good as its weakest link, so an experienced commander would probably take care to place reliable troops at the centre and flanks. Depending on numbers there may have been 2nd and 3rd ranks behind the shield wall, which could have still thrust

[35] (Jennings, 2007:152-4)
[36] (Malmesbury, 1989:9)

long spears or used missile weapons such as stones, spears or arrows.

A shield wall formation – Ealdfaeder re-enactors.

To punch through an opposing line, one may form a flying V 'boar's snout' formation, with two doughty warriors at its head, ready to be replaced by their neighbours if they fell. One of the problems encountered at this time was the barrier formed by the dead and wounded falling between the two opposing lines, making it difficult at times to get at each other, or making a retreat difficult. To contain a concerted attack on a section of the line one can arc it inwards, so that the attackers are semi surrounded, but that can then cause problems elsewhere if the ends of the line are outflanked.

The use of archers seems to have been limited at this time to snipers picking off enemies from the edges of the battle, rather than the massed ranks acting in unison in later times to provide an arrow storm. The bow is a specialist weapon, and one needs to train with it regularly to be effective, whereas the spear is cheaply made and relatively easy to learn to use. The ideal long bow was made of yew, capable of anything from 80-100 pounds draw weight, but doubtless hunting bows of other woods and lesser power would be utilised. I know from experience that a 35 pound ash bow I use can cause considerable damage over a reasonable range. One did not have to be too accurate either with so many men closely grouped together; miss one and you hit his neighbour.

Before battle commenced, individuals may detach from the line and go forward to threaten or harass the opponents. A continuous stream of young warriors trying to prove themselves by hurling javelins or using slingshots is demoralising when all you are allowed to do is stay in line with your shield raised over your head until your arm is achingly tired. Inevitably, after a lot of shield beating and threats one side would advance towards the other. I know from re-enactment experience that this is difficult to control without practice. People move at different rates and length of stride, so beating time helps to instil some co-ordination, so long as commands are clear – difficult using just the voice in a noisy situation. Also, remember that many may have had bare minimal or no training: tenants who owed military service may have only just have been called away from their fields, be unfamiliar with combat and not understand or support what they were fighting for. It was a rich leader who could afford a permanently retained dedicated and trained fighting force. As we shall see later, allies called in to assist were not always reliable either!

Later Old Norse sources detail Heathens throwing a spear over the heads of the enemy and dedicating them in death to a war god such as Woden (Odin) or Tiw (Tyr). Whether their Saxon cousins did the same is not recorded, but it may seem likely. A Heathen warrior would probably take a fatalistic view: if I am destined to die today I will, whatever I do. If I fight bravely I may be chosen by the Valkyries for the warrior heave Valhalla. (The Anglo Saxons had an OE word for valkyries, so presumably they had a belief in them to.)

As one side charged they may have thrown a battery of weapons from close quarters. The inevitable spears, but also the *francisca* axe, designed for throwing. It rotated about its own length to provide a considerable missile. Those that fell short bounced up at random angles from the ground to take out the legs of those with their shields raised to protect their bodies. The *francisca* (named after its Frankish inventors) had an effective range of up to 40 foot (12 metres) and could cause mayhem, particularly when thrown in a collective volley.

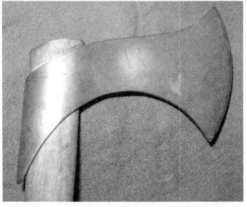

Reproduction war axes: (Left bottom) Early, (Left top) Bearded (right) Francisca

Once a line broke, and hand to hand combat could ensue, other weapons could come into play: the hand axe taken from carpentry tasks is an obvious one. However, it is uncertain whether the bearded axe (with an extended lower edge to hook down shields and weapons) was available in Britain at the time. Certainly the ferocious long handled Dane axe does not appear until much later.

Swords are still a high status weapon at this period, and it has been thought that only a small percentage of warriors would possess one, since they were relatively very expensive. However, Mortimer[37] convincingly argues that the Romans managed to equip each soldier with a sword, helmet and armour, so why not the Saxons who sometimes beat them?

Swords were frequently named and some became family heirlooms. Whilst they may have given status, modern re-enactors have found in practice that a warrior who knows how to use a long spear plus shield effectively can keep another armed with a sword or axe out of reach to cause harm. One would have probably tried to avoid clashing swords with an opponent to avoid damage to sword blades. Being quite heavy the technique was more to get in a blow and back out before the enemy could retaliate. Really important and wealthy leaders such as Penda may have had a better pattern welded sword: twisted rods hammered together to form a patterned, flexible middle with a harder sharpened edge welded on. These cost many years' average wages.

---

[37] (Mortimer, 2011)

Sword types (reproductions, L-R) Early, Seax, 'cocked hat' pommel,'lobed' pommel.

(Above) Pattern welded

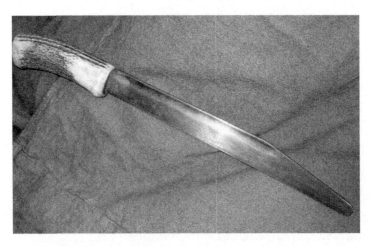

Seax with antler handle (reproduction)

The hilts of early Anglo Saxon swords tend to be partly organic, with wood, bone, leather and antler sandwiched between the metal parts. The tang spike that extended through this handle tended to finish on a washer beaten onto the flat end. Later, the tangs were made longer and bent over to make a stronger finish, so it is then that ornamental caps are used to finish the end. The hilts become all metal, and some have a ring attached to one side of the cross piece. There are arguments as to whether this was for oath taking purposes or simply to anchor a lanyard to prevent loss. Eventually these rings become stylised and solid, negating the latter use.

A weapon close in use to the sword but only single edged was the *seax*, from which the Saxons are believed to get their name. It can be from short sword length down to pocket knife, and could be used as a 'weapon of last defence' if a main weapon was lost. Many were mounted horizontally on the belt, and probably doubled as general purpose tools as well as a stabbing/ slashing weapon in the same style as the Roman *gladius*.

An individual with a sword may also have afforded some more expensive protective armour as well: a helmet and chain mail. Only half a dozen helmets have ever been excavated from this period: the famous ones from Sutton Hoo and Coppergate York, the Wollaston Pioneer helmet, the Benty Grange boar crested artefact and fragments elsewhere in Caenby and the Staffordshire Hoard, boar crests at Guilden Morden Cambs and Horncastle Lincolnshire. Some of these are similar in form to earlier Roman cavalry helmets.[38]

---

[38] (Mortimer, 2011)

Reproduction helmets: Simple, Flapped, Sutton Hoo

The Romans had a form of chain armour, and this seems to have been developed further in the Early Medieval period. It was very labour intensive to make, needing wire to be made, formed into about 30,000 circular links and then for each to be individually riveted or welded. The resultant weight is around 2.5 stones (35 kg) which slows ones movements unless very fit. The weight does spread across the body but I have found in practice with my replica that hitching some over a strong leather belt helps to take the weight off the shoulders. The mail is usually worn over a linen jacket padded with wool, usually referred to as a *gambeson* or *jack.* Whilst a mail coat protects against some cuts, the inner garment protects from bruising and broken ribs as well as forming a cushion layer between mail and skin.

One alternative is to use another Roman invention; lamellar armour, constructed of overlapping fish scale plates of leather or metal. It is thought that the figure on the Repton cross shaft is wearing some.

Above Left: Repton cross shaft, possibly featuring Ædelbald with lamellar armour.

Above Right: Ealdfaeder re-enactor with leather lamellar armour.

Initially chain mail was a good defence against arrows, but fletchers then invented a long narrow bodkin arrowhead to penetrate it. Mail tends not to survive well in the ground, fusing unto an indistinct lump of rusty iron if it survives at all. Its original users must have had to keep it greased to prevent rust while they were wearing it.

Although none to my knowledge have been found to have survived or been identified, it is highly likely that warriors may have protected their right wrist with a leather vanguard or similar, since it is very exposed and vulnerable when one extends the arm with a weapon.

That high status individuals were regularly killed or wounded in battles (whether they be small skirmishes or 10,000 set piece encounters) suggest that leaders like Penda would have been expected to have physically fought, as well as commanding troops, and could not rely upon hiding behind his *housecarl* bodyguards who were expected to protect him. How that was resolved in practice is hard to say.

It is unlikely that he would be encountering the lower orders of warrior: a man dragged off from ploughing a field and given a spear is likely to choose a similar opponent rather than the intimidating heavily armoured elite leader with superior weapons and bodyguards. His outfit alone is a deterrent and says that he is professionally trained for combat. However, I have also found in practice that a person who is well trained to use a long spear can be a formidable opponent. One may have the best of swords and armour, but it is useless if they can hold you six feet away where you cannot reach them. You can try to wipe the spear away or flatten it with a shield but they may counter by slightly withdrawing it and coming back dangerously under it or to the side of it. Not only is it pointed, it has sharp edges to, and a slash to the leg may be the finish of you: either then through falling or bleeding to death, or later through the wound becoming poisoned. Whilst there were herbal poultices and some limited medical assistance available to some, I suspect that many died a lingering death of gangrene or tetanus in those weeks after a battle. It is said that those suffering stomach wounds were sometimes fed onion soup. If the wound started smelling of onions, then it meant that the gut was punctured and medical help would be better directed to victims with a better chance of survival.

Chapter 6 Wars against Wessex & Northumbria.

The un-named sister of Penda was married to King Cenwalh of Wessex. In 645 he rejected her and replaced her with a second wife, which Penda reacted to by forcing him out of Wessex. He must have taken it as a personal insult to his family dynasty and his sister's honour and reputation. Cenwalh took refuge with King Anna of East Anglia for three years, no doubt causing King Anna to be reckoned as an enemy also. We shall deal with the eventual consequences of this in the next chapter.

Quite soon after in 652 Penda was fighting on another front, allied with the Christian Ethelwald, king of Deira who had succeeded Oswine in 642 in Northumbria. Bede says:

> "the hostile army of the Mercians, under the command of Penda, cruelly ravaged the country of the Northumbrians far and near, even to the royal city, which has its name from *Bebba* [i.e. Bamburgh], formerly its queen. Not being able to take it by storm or by siege, he endeavoured to burn it down; and having pulled down all the villages in the neighbourhood of the city, he brought thither an immense quantity of beams, rafters, partitions, wattles and thatch, wherewith he encompassed the place to a great height on the land side, and when he found the wind favourable, he set fire to it and attempted to burn the town. At that time, the most reverend Bishop Aidan was dwelling in the Isle of Farne, which is about two miles from the city; for thither he was wont often to retire to pray in solitude and silence; and, indeed, this lonely dwelling of his is to this day shown in that island. When he saw the flames

of fire and the smoke carried by the wind rising above the city walls, he is said to have lifted up his eyes and hands to heaven, and cried with tears, "Behold, Lord, how great evil is wrought by Penda!" These words were hardly uttered, when the wind immediately veering from the city, drove back the flames upon those who had kindled them, so that some being hurt, and all afraid, they forebore any further attempts against the city, which they perceived to be protected by the hand of God." (BEH)

Bamburgh, Northumberland, from the sea.

One doesn't often associate siege as a method of warfare in Anglo Saxon times, but it was obviously considered here and elsewhere e.g. Siege of Edinburgh. Warfare tends to be described more often as taking place at strategic places in open country such as high ground (at Hatfield Chase) or a river crossing, such as the Battle of the River Idle. Is it because the combatants do not want settlements to be destroyed, or is it because they were hard to defend? As can be seen at Bamburgh, buildings are mainly flammable, unlike the later Medieval stone built houses surrounded by substantial defensive walls. Yes there may be a ditch and earth embankment topped with stakes, but there is little evidence of the early Anglo Saxons emulating their Roman predecessors with a fortified wall (even if they re-used them at times.) However, anyone visiting the rocky outcrop of Bamburgh today can appreciate its' strong defensive position, even without the much later castle built on top. It is defended by the sea on one side, and presents a formidable challenge for warriors to climb, even without the hail of missiles they were likely to receive as their welcome.

Siege warfare can tie up a large number of troops for a considerable time, especially if the defenders have access to food and water. One would imagine that Bamburgh could have re-supplied itself by sea, and there are plenty of natural springs locally. Committing ones army to a siege is acceptable if the commander has a large standing army. It is not so practical if the bulk of one's troops are drawn from farming tenants with an annual duty of military service. They would have to return home at some stage to attend to their work, or starvation for the kingdom will ensue, and no rents or taxes to the king. Whilst Penda would have undoubtedly have attracted a number of professional soldiers and had a personal bodyguard retinue of housecarls, we do not know the composition of his army. All that we do know is that he kept them well employed and busy!

The decision to attack Bamburgh was very significant, according to Brian Hope-Taylor[39] who excavated Bamburgh &

---

[39] (Hope-Taylor, 1977)

Yeavering: it was a twin 7th century capital for Bernicia (by then a part of Northumbria) with Yeavering, which Penda also attacked. Bede says that Edwin had brought Paulinus the missionary to *Ad Gefris* to preach to and convert the local population. *Ad Gefris* has been generally agreed to be the same place as Yeavering. Taylor proposes that this was the centre of power for originally ruling the conquered Britons, whilst Bamburgh was more of a Saxon capital, at a strategic military point on the coast. The queen Bebba (Eobba, Babba) mentioned by Bede was the mother of Ida according to Nennius. Ida was reputed to be the first king of Bernicia.

Yeavering is a very complex site to fully understand, with the ancient 1st century BCE Yeavering Bell hill fort and a Neolithic henge. There is what is presumed to be an Anglo Saxon period Pagan temple, a palace and a unique semi- circular stadium/ amphitheatre with tiered seating and a Christian period cemetery.[40]

It is believed by many that Ethelwald was originally appointed as sub king of Deira by Oswiu of Bernicia when he gained control of all Northumbria by killing his partner king Oswine. However, Ethelwald could have just seized kingship during the vacuum of power left after the battle of Maserfelth, as son of the now dead King Oswald of Northumbria. It could explain why Ethelwald decided to join Penda in these attacks on his supposed mentor's kingdom. Was he revolting against Oswiu as his overlord or dealing with him as a rival? Bamburgh was an important powerbase to be dealt with, on the border of

[40] (Frodsham & O'Brien, 2009)

Deira (often incorporated into Northumbria by this time) which was of strategic importance and controlled merchant shipping on that coast, with the associated revenue from taxes and tolls.

However, in the later Battle of Winwaed Ethelwald withdrew his support of Penda, and later disappears from the records with Alchfrith being installed as king in his place by the victorious Oswiu, who presumably could not trust Ethelwald after his attacks. An unconfirmed tradition says that Ethelwald became a hermit monk at Kirkdale in Yorkshire, so maybe Oswiu allowed this to happen rather than execute him since he had not supported Penda in the final battle.

Chapter 7. Into East Anglia

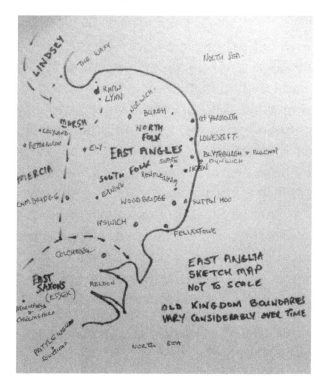

Sketch map of some locations, East Anglia.

In 626 King Raedwald of the East Anglian Wuffing dynasty had been dead for about one year. His son Reginhere had previously died in battle against the Northumbrian King Ethelred on the Mercian border to the East of the River Idle in 616.

Ethelred had tried to bribe Raedwald to give up the fugitive Edwin from shelter at his court, but Raedwald's un-named Queen persuaded him to behave honourably. Subsequently Raedwald assisted Edwin regain his throne, and one would expect Edwin to be grateful and accept Raedwald as his

Bretwalda. After Raedwald died Edwin becomes Bretwalda, with Eorpwald, the second son of Raedwald as his sub king.

King Eorpwald of East Anglia died in 627, to be replaced by his brother Ricbert until 630, then Sigeberht until 640. This Sigeberht had returned from France, having been in exile from his father Raedwald. It is not known why he had fallen out with his father. Sigeberht had met Felix of Burgundy whilst abroad, and invited him to East Anglia. St. Felix, as he became known became Bishop of Dunwich and was partly based at Felixstowe, which bears his name. He also founded a monastery at Soham. Sigeberht eventually gave up the throne to enter a monastery, and handed over authority to a kinsman called Ecgric. Ecgric is also probably known in other sources as Æþelric, the son of Raedwald's brother Eni. He was already a sub king of the kingdom.

Not content with maintaining hostilities against the Northumbrians, Penda also then waged war against East Anglia. He must have been capable of attracting and inspiring a large and effective army of followers: the usual practice was for kings of this period to be given all the spoils of a battle. They could either hoard it all for themselves, or award parts of it to favoured warriors who had given them good service. Hence, the description 'generous ring giver' is one of the highest compliments one could pay a leader of this age. By awarding honour (like a medal but of more practical worth) one received honour in return, and was likely to attract even more keen young warriors to the war band. The honour may even be passed down. A warrior may choose to praise his wife and publicly award her some of his newly gotten arm or finger rings. She could in turn praise her daughter with a gift, and thus increase her marriage prospects. Thus one battle honour could benefit many people, and would increase the status of all of them.

Penda would have needed to employ personal bodyguards, often known as housecarls. These would be well trained and armed, with a duty to loyally protect their leader in public, as well as on the battlefield: assassination of rivals is not uncommon at this time.

With the threat of Penda looming in 640, Ecgric (Æþelric) appealed to Sigeberht to leave the monastery and rally the East Angles, as a proven popular military commander. He refused, and was then forcibly ejected from the monastery, but would only carry a wand as a weapon, and was killed as well as Ecgric in 640. Ecgric had been married to Hereswið of the house of Deira, demonstrating the complex inter relationships between kingdoms when daughters were often given in marriage to strengthen political alliances.

King Anna (alternatively called Onna in the ASC) followed Ecgric as the next of the Wuffing dynasty, and one wonders why Penda did not take control of East Anglia for himself, either directly or by using a puppet king. King Anna's main palace is said to have been at Exning, near modern Newmarket, close behind the Devils Dyke defences. Penda's decision not to rule East Anglia directly is one he may later have regretted when King Anna ruled. However, he did manage to oust him into exile in 651 (in between his campaigns elsewhere) attacking a monastery founded by the Irish at Cnobheresburh.

The church property was taken for safety to France by the Celtic monk missionary Fursey (Fursa) who had created a small monastery at Cnobheresburh in about 631 with his brother Foillan and two priests, Gobban and Dicul. The monastery lay in the North East corner of the ruined Roman built Saxon Shore Fort Gariannonum. Charles Green's excavations in 1959 revealed fragments of painted plaster, Saxon pottery and a Christian burial ground.[41]

Left St. Fursey window, Church of St. Peter & St Paul.
Right: Burgh Castle, Norfolk, home of Fursey.

The castle had been created by Caurasius, Count of the Saxon Shore at Burgh near modern Gt. Yarmouth. A stained glass window in the local round towered church of Saints Peter & Paul commemorates Fursey, based on a miniature from an old manuscript in the British Museum.

Why Penda chose to attack the monastery in about 651 is not clear: he did not seem to attack other monasteries. Maybe it was purely the fact that King Anna was defending it. The monastery was within such a formidable castle defence, a

---

[41] (Milligan, 1983: 3)

major strategic advantage and would have maybe allowed the monks to escape with their relics and treasures.

The case for Cnobheresburh being Burgh Castle is stated by Camden.[42] This has been disputed, but no other major contender has been proposed. It can still be visited today, but no trace of the monastery is visible. There is sometimes confusion about its location, due to the county boundary changes of 1974, which resulted in it moving from Suffolk to Norfolk. It is on the peninsular formerly known as Lothingland and overlooks the river Waveney (which was once much wider) and its joint estuary into the sea with the rivers Yare and Bure.

It has already been stated that Penda had control of East Anglia (and Mercia) in about 626. Was this through sub kings or has Bede made a mistake? Raedwald succeeded King Æþelberht of Kent as Bretwalda on his death in 616, so could not have been subservient to other Kings from 616-625. Did Penda have a claim over Raedwald's successors? By this time Raedwald's protégé Edwin was Bretwalda in Northumbria. Was this an attempt to attack Northumbria indirectly through one of its remoter client kingdoms, or had King Anna done something in his own right to incur the wrath of Penda?

It would seem that in sheltering Cenwalh, the exiled King of Wessex who Penda had driven out for abandoning his sister, King Anna had defiantly harboured a sworn enemy. Bede says that he was sheltered there for 3 years, but his exile had begun in 645. That means he must have sought refuge for 6 years before reaching King Anna's court in 651. Could it be

[42] (Sutton, 2004)

that other rulers would not shelter him for fear of the same fate that met King Anna? Or was Cenwalh sheltered by Anna's predecessor Aethelric, following his Uncle Raedwald's example with Edwin?

King Anna returned from exile two years later. This time Penda killed King Anna and his son Eormen (Jurmin or Iurminus) at the battle of Bulcamp, to the east of Blyford, across the estuary from Blythburgh, Suffolk in about 654. (653 according to ASC) King Anna is thought to have been buried at Blythburgh Priory, (and possibly found more recently by the Time Team TV archaeologists) and remains of the later Augustinian house can still be seen near to the massive church known as 'the Cathedral of the Marshes.'[43] Its' late decorative angels & carvings make it a place well worth exploring.

Bulcamp, near Blythburgh, Suffolk.

---

[43] (Roberts, Montague & Naylor, 1999)

Blythburgh Church angel carving

Both Bulcamp and Burgh Castle are towards the Eastern coast of East Anglia, the traditional powerbase of Raedwald with his palace at Rendlesham. Yet Anna (or Onna) was said to have his base to the far west of the kingdom at Exning, where his daughter Æðelðryð was born. This begs the question as to why Penda's attacks were to the East, unless Anna maintained a second base near to Blythburgh. It could be that he had already been charged to defend the nearby series Devils Dyke ditches at the entrance to East Anglia nearby whilst he was still only Raedwald's nephew, and unlikely to become a king.[44] There are well preserved recent high status Anglo Saxon skeletal finds in Burwell Rd., Exning, including a possible bed burial.

The ASC states that after Cenwalh's period of exile in East Anglia for three years he defeated the Welsh at Penselwood in 658, driving them as far as the Parret. In 661 he is also reported as fighting at Posenesburh. That means he either survived the battle at Blythburgh in 654 or had fled beforehand.

---

[44] (Sneesby, 1999: 3-5)

Icanhoe cross shaft, Iken Suffolk.

ASC says that Botwulf (St. Botolph) began to build a minster at Icanhoh, which may have been to commemorate King Anna. He stayed there until his death on 17th June, 680. His remains were later distributed between Beodricsworth (Bury St Edmunds), and Burgh. The beautifully simple yet atmospheric church of Iken Hoo can still be seen on a promontory of the river Alde. The original wooden one was attacked by Vikings in 870, but it was rebuilt in stone. The modern fabric contains a piece of ancient Anglo Saxon stone cross erected to commemorate the site. It has a coiled dragon, a cross enclosed in a circle and intricate interlace patterns. It is thought that the four and a half foot fragment was once twice as tall.[45] The river Alde flows from Snape where a 14 metre long Saxon boat burial and a large Anglo Saxon cemetery were found, past Iken to Aldeburgh on the coast.[46]

---

[45] (Tricker, 1996:2)

[46] (Filmer-Sankey, 1992:39-51)

Anna's son Eormen who died at Bulcamp is thought to be the same person as St. Jurmin of Beodricsworth (Bury St. Edmunds.) Aethelhere the next brother succumbed in a battle of 655 and the final brother Aethelwald died in 664. It is not known whether Penda set up Aethelhere as a puppet sub king, but given his experience with King Anna it would not have been surprising.

King Anna left four daughters who became acknowledged as saints: Æðelðryð (sometimes referred to as Ethelreda) was born in Exning (where Anna is said to have had a palace) in 630 and married Tondberht, ealdorman of the South Gyrwas in the Fens. On his death in 655 she went into a nunnery at Cratendune near Ely, but was not to be left in contemplation for more than five years. In 660 she was married to the 15 year old Ecgfrið who became King of Northumbria, as a way of Oswiu consolidating power in a Northumbrian – East Anglian alliance against the power of Mercia. However, Bishop Wilfred later encouraged her to enter the Northumbrian monastery at Coldingham, having dissolved her marriage to the much younger king (who had an alternative partner Eormenburga in mind) from where she later returned to her East Anglian roots to found an Abbey at Ely.[47]

Æðelðryð's three sisters were Seaxburh (improbably also known as Seaxburga!), Æðelburh (Ethelburga) and Wihtburh (Withburga). They also all went on to have noted lives:

Seaxburh married King Eorcenberht of Kent, and founded a monastery at Sheppey. After her husband's death she went to be an Abbess at her sister's foundation at Ely.

_____

[47] (Points, 2008:29-30)

Æðelburh went to a double monastery in Northern France called Faremoutiers-en-Brie, which was run by her step sister by her mother's previous husband, Seðryd. She eventually took over as Abbess herself.

Wihtburh founded a Nunnery at Dereham, Norfolk and a well in the churchyard is named after her. As a saint her bones were later moved to Ely.

Chapter 8 Heathenism and the introduction of Christianity to Mercia.

Nobody knows for certain which gods and goddesses Penda acknowledged. The likely main ones are Woden, Thunor, Ingvi-Frey, Tiwaz (Tiw), Frea (Freyja) and Frigga, but he had a large number to choose from. He may also have known them by slightly different regional dialect names (such as Grim for Woden) or had allegiance to a particular lesser known deity such as Seaxnut.

Herbert[48] cites the 13th century Englisc poem 'Brut' written by Layamon in the Norman period as evidence for worship of the Goddess Frea on a Friday. Some sources argue the origin of the day as Frigga-day, commemorating another goddess often confused with Frea. Other days associated with specific deities (often corresponding with Roman counterparts of similar attributes) are Tiw's-day, Woden's-day, Thunors'-day and Sataere-day, with the remaining days of the week celebrating the Sun and the Moon. There is also a belief in other supernatural forces, evidenced by the OE words *nihtgenga* (goblins) and *wudu-elfen* (wood elves.)

Our knowledge of Anglo Saxon Pagan practices is fragmentary, and cannot always be relied upon to duplicate its related better known religious practices in the Scandinavian world. As a king Penda would be expected to take a leading part in some religious rites, but would have employed priests and priestesses also. As can be seen in the story of Edwin's conversion, an Anglo Saxon Heathen priest such as Coifi should not ride a stallion or carry a weapon, and no weapons were allowed within a temple. Pollington[49] discussed the OE

[48] (Herbert, 1994: 25)

word *Þyle* as a 'ritual speaker' in comparison with the general word *scop* for a poet / storyteller, and this may well be the term equivalent to the ON *goði* for a Heathen priest. That role included being able to recite and interpret oral law codes, and thus the term *Þyle* may possibly include both those roles also.

The ability to recite would be of immense use to the Heathen magician: the various Anglo Saxon verse charms contained within the *Cotton Vitellius Ciii* manuscript and the *Nine Herb Charm* show the powerful use of words as well as magical herbs. Some did later have a Christian gloss put on them (such as the Aecerbot 'Erce, Erce' crop blessing from the Book of Exeter) but clearly show their Pagan origins not just in their words, but the ritual actions associated with them such as incense, fennel, salt and soap being rubbed onto the plough as part of the charm.[50]

Many of those Anglo Saxon temples were known abroad to be well constructed, and Bishop Mellitus was instructed by Pope Gregory in 601 to convert them into Christian churches rather than destroy them. (BEH) King Sighere of the East Saxons rebuilds some Heathen temples in 665 when he reverts to Heathenism after a devastating plague.

No temple site is mentioned for Penda, but it is likely that one would have been constructed by a palace, such as the ones at Yeavering, Goodmanham and Rendlesham in this period for formal rituals, although there is also the practice of open air celebrations by a *hearg* altar. Some of these sites are identified in place names as 'harrow' such as Harrow on the Hill. Woodlands also appear to have been used as holy sites

---

[49] (Pollington, 2002:58)
[50] (Davidson, 1990:113-4)

e.g. Thunorsley (modern Thundersley, Essex) refers to a clearing in a wood (lea) dedicated to Thunor.

Sacred groves were targeted by King Charlemagne and Bishop Boniface in Germanic/ Frankish areas, some of which contained a sacred pillar known as an Irminsul or Donar's Oak. (Donar is another name for Thor / Thunor.) Wessex born Boniface cut down one at Fritzlar and Charlemagne is credited with the destruction of one at Heresburg (now Obermarsberg, Germany) in the late 8th century. It has been suggested that the place names Stapoll in Bedfordshire and Stapleford, Leicestershire refer to a 'sacred pillar.' Saint Anselm also refers to *ermula* at Pagan shrines in Wessex, and the pillars may possibly represent the mythological Yggdrasil world tree supporting the nine worlds.[51]

Ritual feasts of sacrificed animal meat (possibly including horse that was outlawed by Christianity) and ale or mead were probably a major part of ritual activity, along with chants & songs. If Saxons followed Norse example the priest / priestess would have had an arm ring for oaths to be made upon, and from the story of Raedwald a number of idols would have been exhibited. At certain times of year one may have been paraded around in a wagon, if the Saxons continued Germanic custom.

---

[51] (Ellis Davidson, 1990: 190-195)

Reconstruction of spear dance by Ealdfaeder.

Given the numerous spear dancer motifs on the Sutton Hoo helmet, Finglesham belt buckle and their Scandinavian counterparts it is likely that a ritual dance may have been performed, including special helmets and animal disguises.[52] Various laws and bishops edicts specifically ban dressing as animals, saluting the moon, leaving offerings at sacred trees and wells and making sacrifices, so one can conclude that these were all Heathen practices carrying on in England for some centuries after official conversion to Christianity.[53]

Early Norse and Saxon beliefs do not mention a heaven, with immortality going to those who left a strong reputation to be put into song or poetry. Later ideas of Valhalla as a warrior heaven and Frea's family friendly Sessrunner Hall do exist, as

[52] (Jennings, 2007:81-4)
[53] (Jennings, 2007: 54-57)

does the idea of Valkyries (alluded to by the Saxon Wulfstan's 'Wolf' 11th century sermon as *wælcyrian*) selecting the valiant slain warriors.[54]

The use of runes for performing magic and divination in addition to being an alphabet for reading / writing is well attested. The Anglo Saxon Rune Poem is more explicit in the meanings of runes that other rune poem examples from abroad. One wonders whether Penda consulted them (or some other divinatory method) before making major decisions. Whilst Page[55] urges caution in how far we give modern magical interpretation to the use of runes, I personally believe that archaeological evidence such as the religious slogans inscribed on objects e.g. 'alu' on the Spong Hill pot[56] and entire futhorc rows on other objects indicate to the contrary. Certainly Old Norse sources as well as the Roman Tacitus describe magical usage of runes. .

Although a Heathen himself, Penda is noted for not objecting to the English and Celtic missionaries visiting his kingdom, or it seemed his own son and daughter converting to the new faith. His son Peada was baptised in 653 by Finan, St. Aidan's successor at Lindisfarne.[57] The Scot/Irishman Diuma was made Mercian bishop soon after the death of Penda, and another English member of the mission called Cedd was sent to the East Saxons, where he became bishop. The remains of his church and monastery can be found in the ruins of the Roman Othona sea fort which can still be visited at Bradwell-

---

[54] (Davidson, 1990:61)
[55] (Page,1987: 15-16)
[56] (Pollington, 1995: 76)
[57] (Blair, 1997:125)

on-Sea in Essex. The fort itself has been half lost to the sea, and the beautifully simple church of St. Peter-on-the-wall is built over the ruins of the old gatehouse

St Cedd's chapel at Othona, Bradwell on Sea, Essex.

AT this time, the Middle Angles, under their Prince Peada, the son of King Penda, received the faith and sacraments of the truth. Being an excellent youth, and most worthy of the title and person of a king, he was by his father elevated to the throne of that nation, and came to Oswiu, king of the Northumbrians, requesting to have his daughter Elfieda given him to wife; but could not obtain his desires unless he would embrace the faith of Christ, and be baptized, with the nation which he governed. When he heard the preaching of truth, the promise of the heavenly kingdom, and the hope of resurrection and future immortality, he declared that he would willingly become a Christian, even though he should be refused the virgin; being chiefly prevailed on to receive the faith by King Oswiu's son Aifrid, who was his relation and friend, and had married his sister Cyneherga, the daughter of King Penda.

Accordingly he was baptized by Bishop Finan, with all his earls and soldiers, and their servants, that came along with him, at a noted village belonging to the king, called At the Wall. And having received four priests, who for their erudition and good life were deemed proper to instruct and baptize his nation, he returned home with much joy. These priests were Cedd and Adda, and Betti and Diuma; the last of whom was by nation a Scot, the others English. Adda was brother to Utta, whom we have mentioned before, a renowned priest, and abbot of the monastery of Gateshead. The aforesaid priests, arriving in the province with the prince, preached the word, and were willingly listened to; and many, as well of the nobility as the common sort, renouncing the abominations of idolatry, were baptized daily.

Nor did King Penda obstruct the preaching of the word among his people, the Mercians, if any were willing to hear it; but, on the contrary, he hated and despised those whom he perceived not to perform the works of faith, when they had once received the faith, saying, "They were contemptible and wretched who did not obey their God, in whom they believed." This was begun two years before the death of King Penda.

(BEH Book 3 XXI)

That last sentence would date this period to finish around 653. It seems to emphasise that Penda was not against Christians, just those who failed to live up to their faith. However, whether Penda was aware of the political advantage that Oswiu may be gaining by sending missionaries into his territory is unclear: he may not have been so used to religion being so closely allied to politics. Fox queries whether Oswiu being able to send missionaries into Mercia may show that Oswiu had power over him, and that Penda was not without problems in the defence of his own kingdom from other kings, including the co-ruler in the north, Eowa.[58] One may wonder at his decision to elevate his son to the throne of the Middle Angles, a part of his larger kingdom. Could it be a general preparation for him to already be accepted as successor to the whole realm when Penda eventually dies?

Tyler[59] presents a worthwhile point:

> That Penda was in a position to install Peada in this way suggests that his interest in and influence among the Middle Angles considerably antedated 653. It is possible that some of the conflicts between Penda and various East Anglian rulers were caused by rivalry over the tributes of the Middle Anglian groups, and the creation of a kingdom here may have been intended to help strengthen Penda's control over these peoples

The magnificent Bewcastle cross commemorates Alchfrith. The son of Oswiu, Aifrid (or Alchfrith) was instrumental in the conversion of Peada, and later fought at his father Oswiu's side at the battle of Winwaed. Herbert[60] believes that he must have been the son of his first wife, the British princess Riemmelth, since if he was the son of the second wife Eanfled of 642 he would only been about eleven years old at the time of the battle. The first wife is not named by Bede, but is named by Nennius and the Durham *Liber Vitae*. She is thought to be a descendant of King Uriens, who Mallory had married off to Morgan le Fay in his Arthurian tales. He led a trio of other

---

[58] (Fox, 2008:15-21)
[59] (Tyler, 2005:7)
[60] (Herbert, 1975)

Northern kings on an assault of the Bernician (later Northumbrian) Bamburgh fortress, but was murdered by one of them before he could succeed.

A man called Chad was a pupil under St. Aidan at Lindisfarne, one of four brothers active in the early church. After broadening his education in Ireland he succeeded his older brother Cedd (see above) as Abbot of Lastingham in Yorkshire. This is the same Cedd who was a priest to Peada. Later in 666 Chad was made Bishop of the Northumbrians, and was based in York. However, due to some controversy over his ordination he was first removed, then re-consecrated and sent to the rival Mercia. In 669 he based himself in Lichfield, a Mercian royal powerbase for the Christian son of Penda, King Peada.

Chad was only there 3 years until dying of plague on 2nd March 672, but in that time he gathered a strong reputation as an evangelist, converting and baptising many people of Mercia, some of them in the nearby Stowe Pool. This must have also increased his sponsors political position and wealth, with so many people making pilgrimage to visit St Chad, or later his shrine.

Chad also had a reputation for studying and praying whenever he could with seven or eight followers at a house near St Mary's Church (on the site of the present cathedral). There was also a tale about his humility, preferring to go on foot than the horse provided for him by Archbishop Theodore, who eventually pushed him up onto it himself and ordered him to use it. (*BEH*)

His tomb became a shrine and a cult of St. Chad grew up around it, and one can still visit St Chad's Head Chapel in Lichfield Cathedral.

St Chad's chapel roof boss showing Theodore giving him a horse: Lichfield Cathedral, Staffordshire.

The shrine was beautifully decorated, and at one time had two 8th century illuminated vellum gospel books enclosed within in it. One of them, known as St. Chad's Gospel has survived, contains Matthew, Mark and part of Luke Gospels, written in Latin, but of a distinctly British origin. It has been calculated that about 100 cattle would have been needed to supply sufficient vellum for the two books, which were originally likely to have been bound in precious jewelled covers. Due to some of the earliest written Welsh language notes inserted in the margins, it is believed that the books were produced in Wales. Did Peada or his descendants who inherited some of his father's Welsh allies play a part in this? We are unlikely to find out, but the books would have been an extremely valuable gift.

Yet another wonder is the limestone carving of an angel, discovered under the nave and believed to be an end panel of the chest containing the saint's relics.[61] St. Chad is known to have visited Tamworth, and a century later it in turn became the seat of Mercian power under the mighty King Offa. St. Editha's church is believed to be on the site of the original one that stood there. It was named for the sister of Aethelstan who was married off to the Dane Sigtrygg as part of a peace treaty. He later reverted to Paganism and she became a nun and established a convent in Tamworth.

---

[61] (Wilcox, 2011)

Lichfield Cathedral, Staffs: (above) St Chad's Gospel

(Below) Angel carving thought to be part of Chad's shrine

Chapter 9 The Final Showdown and tangled family connections.

The Battle of Winwaed (or Winwidfeld/ Wingfield) was fought by Penda to the East of Loidis (Leeds) on 15th November 654. The site is believed to be between Seacroft, Grimes Dyke and Dyke Farm.[62] The river Cock Beck had been swollen with rain and burst its banks.

The recent find of six high status objects known as 'The West Yorkshire Hoard' is said to have been found near Leeds (Loidis). It includes some beautiful gold rings. The battle may possibly explain their presence, since they are of 7th century origin.

King Oswiu his adversary was the father in law of Penda's son Peada. Peada must have felt much divided loyalties between his father and his father in law. Similarly, Ealfrid, son of Oswiu was married to the Cyneburh, the daughter of Penda, and sister of Peada. Presumably she had also converted to Christianity to enable her marriage to take place, with her father's agreement at a time when relationships between the two kingdoms of Mercia & Northumberland were more cordial. Had she (like many royal brides) been destined to be a 'peace weaver', a familial link between the two kingdoms to ease political strife? We do not know.

What we do know is that the man who later became St. Cuthbert left the Melrose monastery to do military service for Edwin at the battle of Winwaed. He returned safely to the monastery afterwards, and became the Prior. He later moved to the Lindisfarne Holy Island monastery as the Prior there,

---

[62] (Wilkinson, 1980:4-9)

and later (after a period as a hermit) as Bishop. He died in about 698 and was buried at Lindisfarne. However, his remains were moved to Durham Cathedral in 1104 to avoid harm by Viking raiders. In the coffin was found his St John's Gospel book, bound in tooled red leather. It is the earliest intact European book, and a £9million bid is being made to buy it for the nation from the Jesuits who have owned it since the Reformation. It is currently held at the British Library but may be exhibited at Durham in the future.

Oswiu had been out manoeuvred by Penda at Iudea, thought to be on the river Forth in Stirlingshire[63]. Oswiu had tried unsuccessfully to buy off Penda with gifts, which hints at Penda's powerful position, and an army alleged to be three times the size of Oswui's. Reportedly Penda eventually accepted an enormous amount of treasure, but then gave the lot to his Welsh allies. Nennius names it by its Archaic Welsh title as 'Atbret Iudea – the Restitution of Iudeu.'

One of Oswui's sons, the ten year old Egfrith was being held hostage at the court of Penda's Queen Cyneswid in Mercia. The taking of hostages to ensure compliant behaviour from defeated or tributary kings was common at this time. Whilst the subject king obeyed, the life of the hostage (often a son or close relation) could be quite comfortable, similar to being honourably fostered, but their fate could be uncertain if the deal was reneged upon. It is likely that Penda would have had many hostages from the courts of kings who were either tributary kings (in some cases set up by him) or defeated ones he wanted to keep in order.

---

[63] (Herbert, 1986:19-21)

Tributary kings would often be given valuable gifts. Whilst this would enhance their status, particularly if the goods were foreign high status objects that they would not be able to obtain by their own personal connections; it would mean that they could be expected to attend the over-kings court, and maybe give him military assistance on his campaigns. Having said that, on balance the over-king (possibly *Bretwalda* if he commanded enough Southern English kingdoms) was then likely to provide extra security in defending his client kingdoms from outside aggression, and boosting his own chances of overcoming kings with larger armies than his own from Mercia, with consequent opportunities for gathering more war booty.

Bede omitted Penda and others from his list of Bretwaldas. This is probably because of his prejudice against Pagans and Mercians, as well as Christians he regarded as heretical i.e. Celtic rather than Roman style Christians, but it seems in reality and effect, Penda was a *Bretwalda* in that he seemed to have exerted influence or conquered a number of other kings. No one is exactly sure of how a king became one, or even if the term was used at the time, but all indications point to royalty who had power over the major part of English kingdoms.

Tyler[64] makes a good case for Penda having influence for at least part of his reign from the coast of Wessex up to Bernicia, including Lindsey, East Anglia under Aethelhere, Gwynedd and other Briton Welsh kingdoms, Deira under Osric and Ethelwald, Magonsaete under Merewalh (who was either the son or son-in-law of Penda) and the West Saxons. It is

---

[64] (Tyler, 2009)

admitted that he did not hold all of them all the time, but even when he did not they must have feared him.

Aethelwald, the nephew of Oswiu and king of Deira had deserted his uncle and joined the Mercians and acted as a guide. However, together with the backing of his son Ealfrid, Oswiu somehow defeated Penda's superior forces, killing Penda. As Fox[65] says:

> Penda had defeated Oswiu's brother, Oswald at the battle of Masefeld in 642 and subsequently nailed him to a tree and mutilated the body. This would have been viewed as an outrage by Oswiu, and one that required an answer.

Penda was according to Bede accompanied by 30 divisions, led by 30 other kings & nobles against his old Northumbrian rival Oswiu (reflecting an ability to demand military tribute from other kingdoms.) This may have been an exaggeration to make Oswiu look good. However, Penda was defeated and killed. In a twist of history one of his allies was King Aethelhere of East Anglia, a Christian fighting on the side of a Pagan who had recently killed his brother King Anna. Had he been ally at that time (with hope of a sub-king role) or had he changed sides later? Also on his side (taking the same ally role as his predecessor) was Cadfael ap Cynfeddw, the king of Gwynedd who had taken power on the death of Cadwallon in 635. He survived the battle, having withdrawn from the field of battle with his army the night before, and gained the nickname 'Battle Shirker', a caustic reversal of the meaning 'Battle Chief' of his name. Eathelwald, who had joined Penda

---

[65] (Fox, 2004:25-7)

in 652 was at the battle, but is also said to have withdrawn to a place of safety during the battle.

Death of Penda – stained glass Worcester Cathedral.

The rout of Penda's forces was made worse by the terrain, as many of them drowned in the river Winwaed trying to flee the aftermath. As a song of the time says:

In Winwed amne vindicata est caedes Annae:
Caedes regum Sigbert et Ecgrice:
Caedes regum Oswald et Edwin:

At the river Winwed the killing of Ann was avenged.
The killing of kings Sigbert and Ecgrice.
The killing of kings Oswald and Edwin. (trans. Georius)

William of Malmesbury[66] judged Penda in death much more harshly than Bede:

"...Penda, king of the Mercians, that destroyer of his neighbours, that seed-plot of hostility..."

Yet I trust that through the detail of this book one may see that he was much more than that. He was responsible for restraining the heavy influence and territorial ambitions of the Northumbrians over the rest of Gt. Britain, and left a lasting legacy.

"No weary mind may stand against Weird
Nor may a wrecked will work new hope;
Wherefore, most often, those eager for fame
Bind the dark mood in their breasts."
(Excerpt from OE poem The Wanderer)[67]

Having made a vow before the battle, Oswiu sent his daughter Elfled to a monastery at Hartlepool, in the care of Abbess Hilda. She was the daughter of Hereric, a nephew of King Edwin of Northumbria who was exiled and eventually poisoned at the court of the Celtic King Cerdic. Hilda was originally bound at the age of 33 for a French monastery, but was persuaded by St Aidan and her nephew King Aldwulf of East Anglia to start a monastic life by the river Wear. Six or seven years later in about 655 she was made Abbess of Hart Island (Hartlepool.)

In about 657 Oswiu gave land to build a new Abbey at Whitby, on the site of an old Roman signal station called *Stroenæshalch* (Bay of the Beacon). Excavations have indicated that there was probably a small 4-5th century Roman Christian presence on the site, so it was probably

---

[66] (Malmesbury, 1989:43)
[67] (Alexander, 1977: 70.)

appropriate that the new abbey was created there, with the resources of 100 hides of land given by King Oswiu.[68] He was later buried there, along with King Edwin of Northumberland.[69] Bede emphasises how pious he was and worthy of being a saint, but Ziegler[70] points out that Oswui's son Alchfrith and nephew Oethelwald rebelled against him and subsequently 'disappeared' presumed assassinated.

It seems likely that Alchfrith of Deira was the son of Riemmelth, the granddaughter of Thu nap Urien (or Urien of Rheged) mentioned by Nennius.[71] He is probably commemorated on the famous runic Bewcastle Cross in North Cumbria. His wife Cyneburh (Kyneburga) appears on it. It would be unlikely that Oswiu would have erected it to his treacherous son, so maybe the theory forwarded by Bell[72] that his half -sister Aelflaed, Abbess of Whitby may have erected it should be supported..

King Uriens is credited with being married to Morgan le Fay by Mallory, fathering the knight Sir Owen.[73] Uriens was based around Carlisle, and persuaded three other Northern kings (Rhydderch of Strathclyde, Gwallag of Elmet and Morcant of Edinburgh) to attack Bernicia with him. Theodric moved out of Bamburgh to meet him, but was overwhelmed by the opposition. He could not get back to Bamburgh so took refuge on Holy Island (Lindisfarne.) The three day siege never

---

[68] (Wilkinson, 1980:5-6)

[69] (Robinson, C. 2002:26-7)

[70] (Ziegler, 2011)

[71] (Herbert, 1975:8)

[72] (Bell, 2011:16)

[73] (Herbert, 1975:6)

developed into an attack across the causeway though, since one of Uriens' allies, Morcant took an opportunity of close proximity to have him murdered. The alliance broke up in confusion. It must have been a lucky escape for Theodric, who had probably unwisely left a good defensible position.

St. Hilda took on organising Oswiu's Abbey at Whitby in 657, bringing Elfled with her from Hartlepool[74]. The monk Caedmon achieved fame as a composer and singer of religious hymns there.

Given that there were around twenty monastic houses (many of them double segregated houses of nuns & monks) in the Humberside area[75] Whitby had a remarkable tally of bishops taught there. The bishops were Aetla, Bishop of the East Saxons, Bosa Bishop of York, John of Beverley Bishop of Hexham and York, Oftfor Bishop of the Hwicce and Wilfred, yet another Bishop of York. This is a different Bishop Wilfred to the earlier one that Hilda spent a lot of time having heated theological debates with. The standard of learning at Whitby must have attracted a high standard of entrant and ensured their development to have achieved so much success with its monks.

After several years illness, Hilda died at the age of 66 on 17th November, 680 and her bones were later moved to Glastonbury by Edmund 1st. Elfled eventually succeeded Hilda as Abbess in 713.

St. Hilda is best remembered as the host of the Synod of Whitby in 664. It was set up to by Oswiu to decide whether the

---

[74] (Wilkinson, 1980)
[75] (James & Fairbank, 1986:16)

Celtic or Roman systems of Christianity should take precedence: at the time they celebrated Easter as much as one month apart, and there were other anomalies such as the way monk's tonsures (haircuts) were styled. The Roman model won, having a tremendous and lasting impact on English Christianity to this day.

Chapter 10 After Penda: his legacy.

As we have already seen, Peada, son of Penda had converted to Christianity in 651, whilst he was still an Ealdorman. When he inherited the rest of the kingdom of Mercia in 655 he attempted to convert the whole of his kingdom to Christianity, and founded Medehamsted Abbey (named after a spring called Medeswæl), which has now become Peterborough. He entrusted the work to an abbot called Seaxwulf.

Hedda stone, Peterborough Cathedral, Cambridgeshire

Peada was killed a year into his reign, and according to ASC he was betrayed by his Queen Elfieda (Alhflæd), the daughter of the late King Oswald of Northumbria at Eastertide. He was succeeded by his younger brother Wulfhere in about 656. Did Elfieda hold Peada partly responsible for the death of her father, or was there some other motive? Wulfhere or Oswiu could have also had motives, according to Lindsey.[76]

> Three years after the death of King Penda, Immin, and Eafa, and Eadbert, generals of the Mercians, rebelled against King Oswiu, setting up for their king, Wulfhere, son to the said Penda, a youth, whom they had kept concealed; and expelling the officers of the foreign king, they at once recovered their liberty and their lands; (BEH)

Wulfhere completed Medehamsted Abbey, and attended its consecration of what had become St Peters Minster with his younger brother Aethelred and sisters Kyneburga and Kyneswitha. He married Eormenhild, the daughter of the Eorcenberht, the King of Kent.

Florence of Worcester[77] said that Merewalh, a brother of Wulfhere (and thus another son of Penda) ruled Western Mercia i.e. the Magonsæton, but various academics have disputed as to whether he was actually related.

Wulfhere fought against Cenwalh of Wessex in 661, (who must have survived the battle between Penda and his protector King Anna) initially at Pontesbury, and then defeated him at Ashdown. Cenwalh had expelled Bishop Wine of Winchester, who sought refuge with Wulfhere, and purchased the See of London from him, something other churchmen disagreed with. After Cenwalh's death in 672 his queen Seaxburh reigned for a year, proving that some Saxon women did have real power.   Wulfhere gave the captured Isle of

---

[76] (Lindsey, 2004:25-8)
[77] (Stevenson, 1996)

Wight to the King of Sussex, Aethelwald, who he had sponsored for baptism However; he also had more spiritual matters to pursue:

His kingdom of the East Saxons (ruled on his behalf by a pair of sub kings) suffered some form of plague, and his sub King Sighere turned apostate, returning himself and his subjects to their Pagan roots.

> For the king himself, and many of the Commons and great men, being fond of this life, and not seeking after another, or rather not believing that there was any other, began to restore the temples that had been abandoned, and to adore idols, as if they might by those means be protected against the mortality. (BEH)

Originally Sighere had been sent St. Cedd in 653 who founded a small monastery and church at *Ythancestir* (Bradwell on Sea.) Due to his success, a year later he was recalled to Lindisfarne (where he had been taught by the St. Aidan, originally from the Celtic Christian community founded on Iona by St. Columba of Ireland) to be made Bishop of the East Saxons, and returned to turn the wooden church into a more substantial stone structure.[78]

However, relationships could not have been easy: on one occasion according to a legend he scolded the king. He had previously warned him about a relation of king Sighere marrying another family member. He had banned them from the church and asked the king not to visit their house, but Sighere did not comply. Apparently Cedd lowered his staff to show disapproval, and warned him that he would die in that

---

[78] (Carter, 2007)

house. The king asked forgiveness but was later murdered by that relative and his brothers.[79]

In 659 his brother Caelin introduced Cedd to King Aethelwald of Northumbria, who gave him land to start another monastery (assisted by his brother Cynebil) at Lastingham, Yorkshire. In 664 Cedd acted as trusted interpreter at the Synod of Whitby (being fluent in Irish and Latin) but later that year died of a plague. Tragically, thirty monks who visited him from Bradwell all died to, except one young boy.

Sighere's co-King Sebbi stayed Christian, and their overlord King Wulfhere of Mercia sent Bishop Jaruman to bring the other half of East Anglia back into Christianity. When Jaruman also died in 664 Wulfhere obtained a new bishop for Mercia and Lindisfarne. That bishop set up his Episcopal See at Lichfield and became eventually known as St. Chad (the other of Cedd's three brothers.) He also started a monastery at *Ad Barve* (At the Wood) on the land of fifty families given to him by Wulfhere at Lindsey.

Wulfhere and his queen Eormengilda often visited St. Chad at Lichfield. Their two sons were murdered, and they founded a Priory at Stone where they were buried.

With all of this consolidation going on in his kingdom, one may be forgiven for thinking that Wulfhere's final years were peaceful, but he fought Cenfus of Wessex in 675, and died later that year.

Queen Eormengilda went into the monastery of her mother Seaxburga at the Minster of Isle of Sheppey. She eventually

---

[79] (Anon, 2010)

became the Abbess when her mother moved to Ely Abbey. Her mother had been a daughter of King Anna of East Anglia and Queen of Kent with King Eorcenberht until 664 when he died.

The next youngest brother of Wulfhere, Aethelred took over now as king in about 675. He made his young brother Ælfwine sub king of Deira.

Aethelred attacked Jutish Kent in 676, and continued to support the grant to Medehamsted Abbey in about 680 (the year that Hilda of Whitby died.)

He also regained control of Lindsey in 679, by beating his brother in law Ecgfrith at a battle near the River Trent. Aethelred's ally, his eighteen year old brother King Ælfwine was killed there, and the Collingham Jewel, a 7th century pyramid shaped sword ornament found north of Newark in 1999 may have come from his or some other wealthy warriors sword fittings. The single, exquisite yet small jewel was valued at £20,000.[80]

Theodore the Archbishop of Canterbury acted as a mediator to prevent further fighting, and Ecgfrith agreed to pay wergild to Aethelred of Mercia for the death of his brother.

As Points[81] indicates, Queen Æðeldryð, the daughter of King Anna and the widow of Tondberht in 655, (who was ealdorman of South Gwynas) married Ecgfrith before he became king of Northumbria. She had been widowed from Tondberht for five years, and was 29. He youthful husband

---

[80] (Kerr, 2000:8)
[81] (Points, 2009:29)

Ecgfrith was only 14-15 years old, young enough to have been her son. The marriage in 660 at York appears to have been arranged by Oswiu to cement relations between Northumbria and East Anglia whilst suppressing Mercia. It lasted until about 672 when the marriage was dissolved, with her going off to found Ely Abbey and Ecgfrith marrying a second wife, the younger Eormenburga.

Queen Ostritha was originally married to King Eanhere of the Hwicce, and had three sons. They were adopted by her second husband Aethelraed. He had previously been married to Babba, whom Bamburgh was named after.

Ostritha was the daughter of Oswiu and sister to both Ecgfrith and Peada's wife Elfreda. Ostritha was killed by Southumbrian forces in about 695-7. The reasons have never really been explained, but her loyalties must have been tested (and maybe suspected) when her 18 year old brother Aelfwine was killed in battle by her second husband, whilst he was warring against her other brother Ecgfrith of Northumbria.

After Ostritha's death Aethelred abdicated being king in 704, and went to become a monk at Bardney, Lincolnshire. Oswald's bones had been placed there by his wife, and so they both had a connection with the place. Aethelred died there twelve years later, and was buried in 716.

Coenred (son of Wulfhere) was the new king of Southumbria in 702, and took over from Aethelred as king of Mercia in 704. It is said that Coenred was old, and abdicated in favour of Aethelraed's son Ceolred only 5 years later in 709. He went off on pilgrimage to Rome with Offa, and died there. It is possible that he was holding the throne until his predecessor's son was old enough. The son Ceolred is believed to be by

Aethelraed's first wife Babba. It is possible that another son of Aethelred, called Ceolwald may have reigned before Ceolred, but sources are unconfirmed for that happening.

Ceolred fought Ina the King of Wessex in 715 at *Woddes beorge* (Wodens Barrow) which is possibly Wanborough, on the Ermine Street Roman road in Wiltshire. He died the following year. According to a letter to Æthelbald from Boniface, he had seduced nuns and destroyed monasteries and went mad. His burial was at Lichfield.

Ceolred was succeeded in 716 by Æthelbald, the grandson of Eawa who was Penda's brother. Thus Penda's direct male descendant lineage had ended with Ceolred in 716, but the succession was continued by Penda's brother Eawa's line. Penda's sister also provided a line that re-emerged in 796 with the coronation of Coenwulf. (See Appendix iv for diagram of possible Mercian Regnal line.)

Æthelbald had been in exile, and had frequently consulted and stayed with St. Guthlac in the Fens, a hermit monk of Mercian royal lineage. Saint Guthlac was the son of a Mercian nobleman Penwald and his wife Tette. After a life as a soldier he turned monk at Repton when he was 24, and two years later in 699 gained permission to continue with a hermit monk's life at Croyland (Crowland) in the Fens with a boatman Tatwin and a servant Beccelm. He lived a frugal existence with poor health made worse by the damp fenland mists, and complained of being assailed by monsters and demons who hated his worship. He died in 714, and an Abbey was built about half a mile from the cells by Æthelbald in 716, two years after his death. By then Æthelbald had gained the Mercian crown, as predicted by Guthlac, and he was fulfilling a promise.[82]

(Left) Croyland Abbey, Lincolnshire.
(Right) St. Guthlac figure on Masons Stone, Croyland Abbey.

Æthelbald is thought to be the figure of a mounted king featured on a stone sculptured cross from his burial place of Repton in 757. He appears to be wearing lamellar armour rather than chainmail, which is very unusual. Lamellar armour is made of many overlapping pieces of leather or metal platelet, in contrast with metal ring mail which is much heavier.[83] On the other side of the cross is a serpent devouring people,

---

[82] (Swift, 2007)

[83] (Thompson, 2006:33)

thought by some to be a symbol of Hell. He attended the important church synod of Cloveshou in 742.

Æthelbald fought against the Welsh in 743, and in 752 was defeated at Burford by his former ally Cuthred of Wessex. He was later murdered at Seckington, 12 miles from Repton (*Hrewpandum)* where he was buried by St Wystan, who is also buried there, giving his name to the church. Wystan was also murdered in 849, allegedly by Berhtferht (or Beorthfrith.) Berhtferht was the son of King Wigmund, who reigned after King Wiglaf. Both Wiglaf and Wigmund are also buried at Repton in the crypt you may still enter today. It is remarkable that such a small village today contains so many royal tombs, but in its' golden period as a Mercian capital it also had an abbey (founded by Peada and his queen Alfleda) that adjoined the church, later destroyed by Vikings, and later still replaced by a priory. The original abbess was Werberga, and she was later succeeded by Aelfthryth who made Guthlac a monk in 697CE.

(Left) Repton church crypt, Derbyshire.
(Right) Anglo Saxon coffin lid from Repton church.

The royal St. Eadburh (or Edburg) was a daughter of Penda, and is associated with a nunnery at Aylesbury. She was thought to have trained St. Osyth, the daughter of Wilburh (another daughter of Penda) who married King Frithuwold, the founder of Chertsey monastery.[84] A shrine dated to about 1300 is believed to contain St. Eadburh's remains which had been moved from Priory Church Bicester to the Norman church of St. Michaels, Stanton Hardcourt, Oxfordshire. They were moved by James Harcourt (Sheriff of Oxfordshire) thus facilitating their rare survival beyond the destruction of the Dissolution.

However, in 2011 the archaeologist Paul Riccoboni discovered a badly damaged reliquary and lead box holding

[84] (Parsons, 2001:58)

several bones at the Bicester Priory site. He believes they are the relics of St. Edburg, born in about 620 and died 18th July, 650. She is believed to be behind the origins of the village place names Addebury & Edburton in Oxfordshire.[85]

These Christian saints are not the only ones credited as being of Penda's line: The legendary child saint. Rumwald was born to his daughter Cyneburh (Cyneherga?) and her Northumbrian husband Aifrid at Sutton. He allegedly lived three days, preached on the Trinity and predicted he would be buried in three successive places.

Meanwhile in 685, Caedwalla of the Gewissae returned with an army from banishment to the West Saxon kingdom and killed its king, Ethelwalch. After laying waste to the country he was expelled by two military commanders (Berthum and Andhun) who took over the running of the country. Caedwalla kept up his attacks and eventually killed Berthum, and ruled the Gewissae.

Not content with that in 686 he conquered the Isle of Wight, killing the king Arwald and his two sons, who were forced into baptism before being executed. Thus were killed the last officially ancient Pagan royalty of England.

Given that Penda is frequently incorrectly credited with being the last Pagan king of England, fighting against the overwhelming power of spreading Christianity, it is worth reflecting on how the old Heathen practices lingered on at least 30 years after his death, and that the missionary zeal of the early church did not result in an overnight conversion of the English peoples. In fact, English kings and bishops were

[85] (Anon., 2011)

still making laws and writing admonishments against Pagan practices for another four centuries: starting with Theodore's 7th century Penitential, The Council of Cloveshou in 747, King Alfred's Laws of the 880s, King Edgar in 970, King Cnut in 995 and King Æthelred of the early 11th century all tried to stamp out Pagan practices.[86] Of course, modern day Pagans would maintain that they never completely succeeded!

Stenton[87] stated

"The overthrow of Penda meant the end of militant heathenism"

I do not see Penda's wars as 'militant Heathenism' or Pagan crusades: it is obvious from the description by Bede who was understandably biased against him as a Christian Northumbrian that he did not attack Christianity within his own kingdom, let alone other peoples. Indeed he frequently had Christian allies in his wars.

Certainly he was a warlike king, (like most of his contemporaries) and ambitious with it. If he had not have been, it was likely that the powerful Edwin of Northumberland would have annexed Mercia, and probably gone on to dominate the whole of England and Wales. Maybe it was a case of 'kill or be killed?' Penda certainly made some useful pre-emptive strikes, was responsible for the deaths of several kings, seemed to attract unlikely allies and was mostly successful in his battles. I heartily agree with a comment made by Holt[88]:

[86] (Jennings, 2007, 54-6)
[87] (Stenton, 2001)
[88] (Holt, 2010:19)

"With Wessex quiescent and East Anglia subordinate there can be little doubt that Penda was the effective overlord of England south of the Humber."

Appendix i

Approximate timeline of events mentioned in this book.

Approximate Date Common Era	Event
450	Romans abandon Britain. Vortigen invites Hengist & Horsa to act as mercenaries
510	Battle of Badon Hill. Welsh heavily defeat Saxons, some of whom return to Europe.
577	Major Welsh defeat at Battle of Dyrham
593	Creoda dies in battle with Ethelric of Northumbria, who also dies.
598	Aethelfrith of Bernicia defeats Scots & Welsh at Catterick.
599	Rædwald inherits East Anglia on death of his father Tyttla
603	King Æthelfrith beats Scots at battle of Degastán. Usurps brother Edwin.
607	Aethelfrith invades Gwynedd
611	Cynegils succeeds Ceolwulf as King of West Saxons.
613	Battle of Bangor-is-Coed. Aethelfrith defeats Welsh – many monks killed.
615	Major raid on Wales by Saxons, possibly by Cynegils & Cwichelm at Beandun. Edwin of Northumberland marries Cwenburga Aethelfrith conquers S. Rheged and marries Acha of Deira.
616	Death of Æthelberht of Kent. Rædwald of East Anglia becomes Bretwalda King Saebert of the East Saxons dies. Sons Saeward, Seaxraed & Seaxbald inherit. Battle of River Idle: King Æthelfrith of Northumbria & Reginhere of EA die.
617	Edwin conquers N. Rheged, Isle of Man & Elmet
620	Edwin conquers S. Rheged
624	Death of Rædwald of East Anglia. Succeeded by Eorpwald. Edwin of Deira becomes Bretwalda.

626	Penda becomes King of Mercia Assassination attempt by West Saxons on Edwin of Northumbria
627	Pagan Ricberht usurps Eorpwald (who had turned Christian) as King of East Anglia. Edwin of Northumbria converts to Christianity
628	Penda fights Cynegils & Cwichelm of West Saxons at Cirencester.
630	Sigeberht usurps Ricberht as King of East Anglia. St Felix & St Fursey re-converts it to Christianity.
633	Revolt by King Cadwallon of Gwynedd against Edwin. Several defeats. Edwin of Northumberland lands force on Anglesey Cadwallon returns & defeats Penda at siege of Exeter. They form alliance against Edwin. Death of Edwin at Battle of Hæthfelth. Cadwallon claims Deira. Oswald of Bernicia becomes Bretwalda Osric of Northumberland defeated at York by Cadwallon Penda becomes king of a wider kingdom.
635	Oswald kills Cadwallon at the Battle of the Wall (Deniseburn) Heavenfield. Cadfael inherits kingdom of Gwyned.
636	Cwichelm baptised at Dorchester and later dies.
638	Oswald expands his territory into Scotland.
640	Ecgric & Sigeberht of East Anglia die in battle against Penda. Succeeded by Anna.
642	Death of Oswald of Northumbria & Eowa of Mercia at Battle of Maserfelth. Oswiu & Oswine split kingdom of Northumbria between them. Oswiu of Northumbria becomes Bretwalda and marries Eanflaed
643	Penda captures part of Deira + part of Lincolnshire & Elmet. Put them under control of Osric.
645	Penda forces Cenwalh out of Wessex for rejecting his wife (Penda's sister)
650	Nominal date agreed by some experts for deposition of Staffordshire Hoard.

651	Oswiu challenges Oswine for control of whole of Northumbria. Oswine flees but is murdered. Ethelwald set up as sub-king of Deira by Oswiu Cenwalh in exile with King Anna of East Anglia Penda forces Anna of East Anglia into exile.
652	Ethelwald joins forces with Penda and they attack Yeavering & Bamburgh, Northumbria.
653	Peada converted to Christianity
654	Penda kills the returned Anna of East Anglia in Battle of Bulcamp + son Eomen Oswald pays off Penda to lift the Siege of Stirling. Oswiu defeats Penda at Battle of Winwaed. Penda killed, succeeded by son Peada.
655	Æthelhere of East Anglia dies in battle – succeeded by Aethelwald
656	Peada murdered. Wulfhere succeeds him
658	Cenwalh of Wessex defeats Welsh at Posenesburh
661	Wulfhere fights Cenwalh of Wessex at Pontesbury & defeats him at Ashdown. West Saxons then ruled by sub kings Sighere & Sebbi. Sighere returns to Paganism.
664	Mission of St. Chad to reconvert Sighere's Pagans back to Christianity. Synod of Whitby opts for Roman Christianity rather than Celtic. Aethelwald of East Anglia dies.
672	Cenwalh of Wessex dies. Queen Seaxburh reigned after him for a year.
675	Wulfhere fought Cenfus of Wessex and died later that year. Succeeded by Æthelred who attacks Kent.
678	Æthelred beat Ecgfrith at Battle of River Kent
679	Aethelred beat King Ælfwine near the river Trent and took Lindsey
680	Death of Hilda of Whitby
685	Caedwalla of Gewissae attacks West Saxons. Kills King Ethelwalch but expelled by military.
686	Caedwalla conquers Isle of Wight and kills last Pagan Saxon King Arwald & sons.

702	Coenred king of Southumbria.
704	Æthelred abdicates to become a monk. Coenred takes over Mercia.
709	Coenred abdicates in favour of Ceolred
715	Ceolred fought Ina of Wessex at Wanborough
716	Æthelred dies. Ceolred dies: succeeded by Æthelbald who reigns until 757.

Appendix ii

References & Bibliography

Alexander, M. (1977) *The Earliest English Poems.* Harmondsworth: Penguin

Anon. (2010) *St Cedd of Bradwell: Bishop of the East Saxons.* Bradwell: SPQR

Anon. (2011) *Talk explores 'saint's bones' find in Bicester* Bicester Advertiser & Review, 20/11/11.

Bede (735) *The Ecclesiastical History of the English Nation.* (trans. Stevens) London: JM Dent & Sons Ltd.

Bell, L. (2011) *Bewcastle Cross.* Widowinde magazine 1(159)16-17

Blair, P.H. (1976) *Northumbria in the days of Bede.* London: Book Club Associates

Blair, PH. (1977) *An Introduction to Anglo Saxon England.* Cambridge: Cambridge University Press

Blair, PH (1997) *Anglo Saxon England 2nd Edition.* London: Folio Society

Branston, B. (1974) *The Lost Gods of England.* London: Book Club Associates

Bromwich, R. (Ed.) (1961) *Trioedd Ynys Prydein: the Triads of the Island of Britain.* Cardiff

Brooks, N. (2000) *Anglo Saxon Myths: State and church 400-1066.* London: Hambledon Press

Brown, M.P. & Farr, C.A. (2001) *Mercia: an Anglo Saxon kingdom in Europe.* London: Leicester University Press/ Continuum

Branston, B. (1974) *The Lost Gods of England.* London: Book Club Associates

Carter, H.M. (2007) *The Fort of Othona and the chapel of St. Peter-on-the-wall, Bradwell-on-Sea Essex.* Bradwell: St Peters Chapel Committee.

Castle, M.A. (2011) *The Parish Church of St Peter & St Paul 26th Edition.* Private:Burgh Castle

Clancy, Joseph (1970), *The Earliest Welsh Poetry* London: MacMillan

Ellis Davidson, HR (1990) *Gods and Myths of Northern Europe.* London: Penguin

Evans, AC (1989) *The Sutton Hoo Ship Burial* London: British Museum

Filmer-Sankey, W. (1992) *Snape Anglo Saxon Cemetery-the current state of knowledge* in The Age of Sutton Hoo (Ed. M Calver) Woodbridge: Boydell

Fox, P. (2004) *The Battle of Winwaed Revisited* in Widowinde magazine 1(133)25-7

Fox, P (2008) *Penda: some unanswered questions.* In Widowinde magazine 1(145)15-21

Frodsham & O'Brien (2009) *Yeavering: People, Power & Place.* Stroud: History Press

Garmonsway, G.N. (1965) *The Anglo Saxon Chronicle.* London: Dent.

Gefrin Trust (2011) http://www.gefrintrust.org/default.htm

George, Dr. K. (2009) *Gildas's De excidio Britonum and the early British church* Woodbridge: Boydell

Giles, J. (1849) *Roger of Wendover: Flores Historiarum* London: Henry J Bohn.

Giles, J. (1841) *The Works of Gildas and Nennius.* London: Henry J. Bohn

Greenway, D. (1997) *Historia Anglorum by Henry of Huntingdon.* Oxford: OUP

Griffiths, B. (1992) *Oswald: Northumbrian king and European saint.* Widowinde magazine 1(94)18-20

Griffiths, B. (1996) *Aspects of Anglo Saxon Magic* Hockwold: Anglo Saxon Books

Griffiths, B. (1998) *An Introduction to Early English Law.* Hockwold: Anglo Saxon Books

Hagen, A. (1992) *A Handbook of Anglo-Saxon Food: Processing and Consumption.* Pinner: Anglo Saxon Books

Hammond, B. (2009) *British Artefacts Volume 1: Early Anglo Saxon.* Witham: Greenlight

Hammond, B. (2009) *British Artefacts Voume.2: Middle Saxon & Viking.* Witham: Greenlight

Herbert, K. (1975) *Haunted Ground.* Widowinde magazine 1(39)4-9

Herbert, K, (1986) *Penda* in Widowinde magazine 1(76)19-21

Herbert, K. (1994) *Looking for the Lost Gods of England.* Hockwold: Anglo Saxon Books

Holt, I (2010) *Penda of Mercia* in Widowinde magazine 1(153)18-19

Hope-Taylor, B. (1977) *Yeavering: an Anglo-British centre of early Northumbria* London: English Heritage

Horn, P. (2011) Early Anglo Saxon England. *Widowinde* magazine 1(159)14-15

Howells & Leonard (2010) *As I heard tell* in Widowinde magazine 1(156)25

Humble, R. (1986) *The Anglo Saxon Kings.* London: Weidenfield & Nicholson

Hywel Fychan fab Hywel Goch of Fuellt (1425) *Red Book of Hergest.* Trans. Rachel Bromwich (2006) *Trioedd Ynys Prydein* Cardiff: Univ. of Wales.

Ingram, J. (1912) *The Anglo-Saxon Chronicle.* London: Everyman Press

James, R. & Fairbank, J. (1986) *Anglo Saxon and Viking Humberside.* Humberside: Humberside County Council Archaeology Unit.

Jennings, P. (2002) *Pagan Paths: A Guide to Wicca, Druidry, Asatru, Shamanism and Other Pagan Practices.* London: Rider

Jennings, P. (2007) *Heathen Paths: Viking & Anglo Saxon Pagan Beliefs.* Milverton: Capall Bann

Kemble, JM (1991) *Anglo Saxon Runes* Pinner: Anglo Saxon Books

Kennedy, M. (2009) *Largest ever hoard of Anglo Saxon gold found in Staffordshire.* In Guardian newspaper, 24/09/2009

Kerr, L. (2000) *Anglo Saxon Stud found in field* in Widowinde magazine 1(122)8& 11

Kerr, N&M (1982*) A Guide to Anglo Saxon Sites.* St Albans: Granada Publishing

Laing, L&J (1979) *Anglo-Saxon England.* St Albans: Granada Publishing

Leahy, K. (2003) *Anglo Saxon Crafts.* Stroud: Tempus

Lindsell, T. (1992) *Anglo Saxon Runes* Pinner: Anglo Saxon Books

Lindsey, R. (2004) *The Death of King Peada.* in Widowinde magazine 1(134)25-8

Malmesbury, W. (1989) *The Kings before the Norman Conquest.* Trans. J Stephenson. Llananerch Publishers: Llanerch

Marsden, J. (1992) *Oswald's Northanhymbre: the Irish dimension.* Widowinde magazine 1(95)28

Milligan, K&R (2011) *Burgh Castle History and Guide. (4th Impression)* Church of St. Peter & St. Paul: Burgh

Mortimer, Paul. (2011) *Woden's Warriors: Warfare, Beliefs, Arms and Armour in Northern Europe during the 6-7th Centuries* Little Downham: Anglo Saxon Books

Newton, Dr. S (1993) *The Origins of Beowulf and the Pre-Viking Kingdom of East Anglia.* Cambridge: DS Brewer

Newton, Dr. S. (2003) *The Reckoning of King Raedwald.* Brightlingsea: Red Bird

North, R. & Allard, J. (Eds) (2007) *Beowulf & Other Stories: a new introduction to Old English, Old Icelandic and Anglo-Norman literatures.* Harlow: Pearson Education Ltd

Page, RI (1987) *Runes* London: British Museum

Paris, Matthew (1883) *Chronica majora, ed. H. R. Luard,* http://parkerweb.stanford.edu/parker/actions/page.do?forward=home

Parsons, D. (2001) *The Mercian Church* in *Mercia: An Anglo Saxon kingdom in Europe. (Ed. Brown & Farr)* Leicester: Leicester University Press

Pelteret, D. (1995) *Slavery in Early Mediaeval England.* Woodbridge: Boydell Press

Plunkett, S. (2005) *Suffolk in Anglo Saxon Times.* Stroud: Tempus

Points, G. (2009) Æđelđryđ – *Queen and Saint.* In Wiđowinde magazine 1(150)29-31

Pollington, S. (1995) *Rudiments of Runelore* Hockwold: Anglo Saxon Books

Pollington, S. (1996) *The English Warrior from earliest times till 1066.* Hockwold: Anglo Saxon Books

Pollington, S (2003) *The Mead Hall: feasting in Anglo-Saxon England.* Hockwold: Anglo Saxon Books

Pollington, S. (2011) *The Elder Gods: The Otherworld of Early England* Little Downham: Anglo Saxon Books

Roberts, H., Montague, M.,& Naylor B. (1999) *Holy Trinity Blythburgh: Cathedral of the Marshes.* Trinity Church: Blythburgh.

Robinson, C. (2002) *Whitby Headland* in Wiðowinde magazine 1(127)26-7

Rodrigues, LJ (1993) *Anglo-Saxon Verse Charms, Maxims & Heroic Legends.* Pinner: Anglo Saxon Books

Sneesby, N. (1999) *Etheldreda: Princess, Queen, Abbess & Saint.* Haddenham: Fern House

Sorrell, M (1991) *The Battle of Maldon, and the death of the Ealdorman Byrhtnoth.* Leigh on Sea: Sorrell

Stenton, F. (2001) *Anglo-Saxon England, 3rd edition.* Oxford: Oxford University Press

Stevenson, J. (1996) *Florence of Worcester: A history of the Kings of England.* Burnham-on-Sea: Llanerch

Stevenson, J. (1989) *William of Malmesbury: The Kings before the Norman Conquest.* Lampeter: Llanerch

Stone, A. (2011) *Penda the Pagan: Royal sacrifice and a Mercian king.* http://www.indigogroup.co.uk/edge/penda.htm

Sutton, DF (2004) *Camden's Brittania of 1607* (Trans. Holland, P) http://www.philological.bham.ac.uk/cambrit/contents.html

Swift, Rev. S. (2007) *Croyland Abbey* Croyland: Croyland Abbey

Taylor, Dr H.M. (2002) *St Wystan's Church Repton: a guide and history.* St Wystan's Church: Repton

Thompson, A. (2006) *The Repton Warrior* in Wiðowinde magazine 1(140)33

Tomlinson, J. (1882) *Hatfield Chace* Doncaster: Private Edition

Tricker, R. (1996) *St. Botolph's Church Iken.* Privately published: Iken

Turner, S. (1807) *The History of the Anglo Saxons, Vol.2.* London: Longman

Tyler, D. (2005) *An early Mercian hegemony: Penda and overkingship in the seventh century*
http://www.e-space.mmu.ac.uk/ e-space/bitstream/2173/14253/2/An%20Early%20Mercian%20Hegemony.pdf

Underwood, R. (2006) *Anglo-Saxon Weapons & Warfare* Stroud: Tempus

Whitelock, D. (1952) *The Beginnings of English Society.* Harmondsworh: Penguin

Wilcox, Rev. Dr. P. (2011) *The Gold, the Angel and the Gospel Book.* Lichfield Cathedral: Lichfield.

Wilkinson, I (1980) *The Monastery of Stroenæshalch & its place in history.* in Widowinde magazine 1(56)4-9

Wilkinson, I. (1980) *Hilda, Abbess and Saint.* in Widowinde magazine 1(57)5-6

Wood, M. (2005) *In Search of the Dark Ages.* London: BBC Books

Zalluckyj, S. (2011) *Mercia: the Anglo Saxon Kingdom of Central England.* Logaston: Logaston Press

Some useful websites

Bede's World http://www.bedesworld.co.uk

British Museum http://www.britishmuseum.org

Ealdfaeder Anglo Saxons http://www.ealdfaeder.org

English Companions http://www.tha-engliscan-gesithas.org.uk

Friends of West Stow

http://www.oldcity.org.uk/stowfriends/index.php

Pete Jennings http://www.gippeswic.demon.co.uk

Steve Pollington http://www.stevepollington.com

Sutton Hoo http://www.nationaltrust.org.uk/main/w-vh/w-visits/w-findaplace/w-suttonhoo

Sutton Hoo Society http://www.suttonhoo.org

West Stow

http://www.stedmundsbury.gov.uk/sebc/play/weststow-asv.cfm

Wuffing Education http://www.wuffings.co.uk/education

Yeavering http://www.gefrintrust.org

Appendix iv

Possible Regnal Line of Mercia

Woðen > Weoðulgéot > Wihtlæg > Wermund > Offa > Angengéot > Eomer > Icel > Cnebba > Cynewald > Creoda (586-593) **> Pybba** (593-600) **> Cearl** (600-615)*

Penda (625-655 South) co- kings **Eowa** (615- 642 North)

Peada (655-656 Sub king under Oswiu of Northumbria until his murder?) >

Wulfhere (658-675) **> Æþelræd** (675-704) > Coenred (704-709) >

Coelræd (709-716) >

After this, the Iclingas line switches from the direct descendants of Penda to other descendants of his father Pybba: his son Eowa and his un-named daughter.

Coelwald (716) **> Aethelbald** (716-757) **> Beornred** (757) **> Offa** (757-796) **> Egfrith** (796) **> Coenwulf** (796-821) **> Cenelm** (821) **> Ceolwulf I** (821-823) **> Beornwulf** (823-825) **> Ludecan** (825-827) **> Wiglaf** (827-828) >

Under Wessex Rule 828-830, then back to Mercian Rule

Wiglaf (again 830-840) **> Wystan** (840) **> Beorhtwulf** (840-852) >

Burghred (852-874) >

Sub-King under Norse Rule

Ceolwulf II (874-879) >

Ruled on behalf of King Alfred the Great of Wessex

Duke Aethelred II (879-911) His Queen, **Æthelfleda** (daughter of **Alfred**) ruled in his stead during his years of illness from 902 and after his death until 918, when she herself died. Her daughter **Ælfwynn** continued on for a while but was deposed by her uncle, **Edward the Elder** the son of Alfred and brother of her mother. It is unusual for Queens to be in control of a kingdom in the Anglo Saxon period.

Queen Æthelfleda, & her daughter Ælfwynn, Tamworth, Staffordshire.

*Nennius gives an alternative genealogy: Woden, Guedolgeat, Gueagon, Guithleg, Guerdmond, Ossa, Ongen, Eamer, Pubba (Pybba)

Printed in Great Britain
by Amazon

36561424R00076